I0532034

Their Story Isn't Over

Prayers, Scriptures, and Hope for Parents and Grandparents of Prodigals

Joanne Beepot

Virtue Publishing

Their Story Isn't Over
Prayers, Scriptures, and Hope for Parents and Grandparents of Prodigals

Disclaimer

Table of Contents

Introduction:
You Are Not Alone

If you are reading this book, it likely means someone you love is far from home—not only from your house, but from the God who loves them most. Perhaps it is your child, the one you cradled, prayed over, and dreamed about. Perhaps it is your grandchild, the one you long to see walk in faith and live with joy. Whoever your prodigal is, the truth is the same: when they wander, your heart aches in ways words can barely describe.

When we speak of a prodigal, we're not just recalling the young man in Jesus' parable (Luke 15) who demanded his inheritance, ran away, and wasted everything before returning in shame. A prodigal is anyone who has drifted from God—through rebellion, addiction, anger, unbelief, destructive choices, or a slow fading of faith.

It may be a teenager experimenting with drugs or alcohol, an adult child trapped in addiction or toxic relationships, or a loved one who has quietly stepped away from church and truth. Whoever they are, a prodigal is simply someone you love who is far from God, and for whom you carry a deep burden of prayer.

Having a prodigal is not a reflection of your parenting, your love, or your faith. It does not discriminate. It crosses every social, cultural, and financial boundary. The pain of watching someone you love wander from God touches every neighborhood, every church, every family. It is the great equalizer of heartbreak. It reminds us that no heart, no matter how strong or successful, is beyond its reach—and none is beyond God's mercy.

1

There is a grief that comes with prodigals, but it is not a grief with closure. It is the ache of birthdays marked by empty chairs, of conversations replayed again and again, of prayers whispered into the night. It is waiting at the window, wondering if the phone will ring, if the car will pull in, if today will be the day they come home.

Beyond grief lies fear: fear of choices made, of friends influencing them, of drugs, violence, accidents, or jail cells. Fear that the story might not end the way you long for it to.

Then comes shame. Perhaps you've felt judged by others who whisper, "If it were my child, that would never happen." Or perhaps you judge yourself, questioning every decision, every word, every moment of parenting or grandparenting. But hear this clearly: you are not to blame for every choice your prodigal makes. God gave them free will, just as He gave you. We can guide, but we cannot control the soul of another.

The Bible is not silent about prodigals. From the beginning, Adam and Eve watched their son Cain choose jealousy and violence. King David's beloved son Absalom rebelled and raised an army against him. The prophet Hosea lived through betrayal as a living picture of God's love for a wandering people. And Jesus told of a prodigal son who squandered everything, yet was still pursued by a father's love (Luke 15:11–32).

You are not walking an unfamiliar road. You are walking an ancient one. And more importantly, you are not walking it alone. The Lord is with you. He sees your tears (Psalm 56:8). He draws near to your broken heart (Psalm 34:18). He will never leave you or forsake you (Hebrews 13:5).

This book was written for you: the weary parent, the heartbroken grandparent, the one ready to give up hope. Each chapter will help you lay down shame, cling to God's promises, pray with authority, and take practical steps to guard your family while waiting for your prodigal to return.

2

It is not a quick-fix guide. It is a companion for the journey. Here you will find Scriptures to hold when faith feels fragile, prayers to pray when words run dry, affirmations to declare when doubt grows loud, and tangible guidance for the hardest seasons.

Take a deep breath. You are not abandoned. You are not unseen. God is at work—even now, even here, even in this season. Though your prodigal may be far from you, they are never far from Him.

Because the Father who ran to embrace the prodigal son in Luke 15 is still running today. He is still pursuing your child, your grandchild, your family. He has not given up. He has not turned away. And He never will.

So, hold fast. Wipe your tears, lift your eyes, and steady your heart. Your prayers are powerful. Your faith is seen. Your prodigal is loved. And their story, no matter how far they've run or how broken the path, isn't over.

Take a deep breath, open your heart, and prepare for this journey of faith and hope. Now, let's begin.

Prayer of Complete Blessing and Restoration

Heavenly Father,

I come before You today, lifting my prodigal to You. You know their name, their story, their struggles, and their destiny. I surrender them fully into Your hands, believing that You love them even more than I do.

Lord, I ask that You break every chain of darkness, addiction, rebellion, shame, and unbelief that holds them captive. Release them into freedom through the power of Jesus' blood. Surround them with people who speak truth and love into their lives. Protect them from the enemy's schemes and from their own destructive choices.

I declare that no curse, sin, failure, or mistake has the final word—Jesus does. Their story is not over. Their future is not ruined. Their hope is alive because You are alive.

I bless my child, my grandchild, my prodigal, in the mighty name of Jesus—with peace that surpasses understanding, with protection that shields their heart, with grace that covers their past, and with faith that anchors their future.

Thank You, Lord, that You are faithful. Thank You that my prayers matter. Thank You that Your promises are true. I trust You with my prodigal's story, and I trust You with mine.

In Jesus' name, Amen.

Part I:
The Weight of the Journey

Every story of a prodigal begins with love, and love often carries both beauty and pain. The waiting, the praying, the heartbreak, and the silence can feel unbearable at times. Yet even here, God is near.

These opening chapters will help you face the ache with faith, release the guilt you were never meant to carry, and remember this truth: your tears are seen, your prayers are heard, and your hope still matters.

Chapter 1:
When Your Heart Breaks

The pain of loving a prodigal is unlike any other. It is grief, but not the finality of death. It is sorrow, but with no clear end. It is waiting without knowing whether the waiting will ever bring what you long for. Your heart breaks in pieces you never knew could be shattered, and yet you still have to rise each morning and live.

Perhaps you've stood in the doorway watching your child leave, wondering if you'd ever see them again. Perhaps you've answered a phone call you dreaded, or watched your grandchild make a choice that fills you with fear. Maybe you carry the ache of silence—the absence of visits, the distance of strained words, the birthdays forgotten, the family gatherings where their absence speaks louder than anything else.

It is natural in those moments to ask: *Where did I go wrong? What could I have done differently? Why is this happening to us?* The enemy loves to whisper lies into those questions. He tells you that you failed, that you are to blame, that your prayers don't matter. But God's truth speaks louder: "There is therefore now no condemnation for those who are in Christ Jesus" (Romans 8:1).

Your broken heart is not evidence of failure; it is evidence of love. You grieve deeply because you love deeply. And God, who is love itself, understands that ache better than anyone.

Think of David, weeping over Absalom. Though Absalom betrayed him, David's cry was still, *"O my son Absalom, my son, my son*

6

Absalom! Would I had died instead of you" (2 Samuel 18:33). Or think of the father in Jesus' parable. Though his son demanded his inheritance and wasted it in reckless living, the father still watched the horizon, longing for the day he would return. And when he finally did, the father ran—not with anger but with compassion.

Friend, your broken heart is not the end of the story. Brokenness is often the place where God does His most powerful work. A heart laid bare before Him is soil where hope can grow again.

Practical Guidance

1. Remember you are not condemned; your pain does not equal failure.

2. Share your grief honestly with God in prayer.

3. Allow yourself to grieve; tears are not weakness.

4. Reach out for support from safe, trusted friends.

5. Give yourself permission to rest; grief is exhausting.

Prayer

Father,

You see the cracks in my heart. You see the tears I hide from others and the weight I carry when no one is watching. You know how deeply I love this child, this grandchild, and how deeply it hurts to watch them wander.

I lay my grief before You. I bring You my anger, my sorrow, my guilt, and my fear. I don't want to carry these burdens alone. I know that You are close to the brokenhearted and that You rescue those crushed in spirit. Rescue me today, Lord.

When I am tempted to blame myself, remind me that You are the Savior, not me. When I am tempted to give up hope, remind me that You are the God of resurrection. When I feel I cannot take another step, hold me in Your strength.

I release my prodigal into Your hands again. I cannot follow them into the far country, but Your Spirit can. Surround them with Your love. Whisper truth into their heart. Protect them in their wandering, and draw them back to You.

Comfort me with Your presence. Hold me when I am weary. Teach me to trust You even when my heart is broken.

In the mighty name of Jesus, Amen.

Affirmations

Speak these truths aloud each day, even when you don't feel them:

1. God sees my tears, and none of them are wasted.

2. The Lord is near to my broken heart and saves me when I feel crushed.

3. I am not to blame for every choice my prodigal makes.

4. My child is never out of God's reach.

5. I may feel powerless, but my prayers carry the power of heaven.

6. My brokenness is not the end; it is where God's healing begins.

7. I will not live in shame; I will live in hope.

8. God is holding both me and my prodigal in His hands right now.

9. What the enemy meant for harm, God can turn for good.

10. This story is not finished—God's redemption is still possible.

Prayer Focus

- Pray for God to strengthen your heart to endure this journey.

- Ask Him to remind you daily that He is near to the brokenhearted.

- Thank Him that He loves your prodigal more than you ever could.

A Letter of Eternal Hope

My Dear [Child's/Grandchild's Name],

My heart aches for you every day, but my love for you never fades. No matter where you are or what you've done, you are still my child and always will be.

More importantly, you are God's child. He loves you beyond measure. Even when you feel lost, He sees you. Even when you feel unworthy, He calls you His.

I will never stop praying for you. I will never stop believing that your story is not over. One day, I believe with all my heart, I will see you walk in the fullness of who God created you to be.

Always love you. Always here for you.

[Your Name]

Chapter 2:
Trusting God's Perfect Timing

Waiting is one of the hardest parts of loving a prodigal. Days turn into weeks, weeks into months, and sometimes years slip by with no change, no breakthrough, no sign of return. You pray and pray, yet it feels as though heaven is silent. You long for a phone call, a visit, a moment of repentance—but instead, you are met with silence or more painful news.

In those moments, it's tempting to believe the lie that God has forgotten you, that He has turned His face away. But the truth is this: God is never late. His timing is not our timing, yet His ways are always higher and His purposes always sure.

Ecclesiastes reminds us, *"For everything there is a season, and a time for every matter under heaven"* (Ecclesiastes 3:1). Habakkuk 2:3 declares, *"For still the vision awaits its appointed time; it hastens to the end— it will not lie. If it seems slow, wait for it; it will surely come; it will not delay."*

Waiting is not wasted time in God's kingdom. While you wait, He is working—both in your heart and in the life of your prodigal. Sometimes He allows delays so that pride can be broken, idols shattered, or circumstances arranged to bring your prodigal to the end of themselves, where they are finally ready to look up.

Think of the prodigal son in Jesus' story. The father waited. He did not run after his son to rescue him from consequences. He trusted that the son's hunger, pain, and brokenness would one day

10

bring him home. And when that moment came, the father was ready—watching, waiting, running with compassion.

Trusting God's timing doesn't mean you stop praying or that you no longer care. It means resting in the truth that the God who knit your child together knows the exact moment, the exact place, and the exact circumstances that will bring them to their senses. You do not have to force the miracle; you only have to trust the Miracle Worker.

Practical Guidance

1. **Release the Clock**
   Stop setting deadlines for God. Instead of "By Christmas, Lord," or "Before they turn twenty-one," release the *when* and *how* into His hands.

2. **Use the Waiting to Grow**
   Let this season deepen your prayer life, your dependence on God's Word, and your compassion for others. Waiting can refine your spirit; it is never wasted.

3. **Mark Small Mercies**
   Keep a journal of every sign of hope—a text message, a brief conversation, a kind word, or even a stirring in your own heart. These reminders strengthen faith in the waiting.

4. **Resist Comparison**
   Other families may see breakthroughs sooner, but God's story for your family is unique. Focus on His timing for you, not theirs.

5. **Guard Against Despair**
   When discouragement sets in, speak Scripture aloud: *"Those who wait for the Lord shall renew their strength"* (Isaiah 40:31). Waiting is not passive despair—it is active hope.

11

Prayer

Father,
You know how weary I grow in the waiting. My heart longs to see change, and yet I confess that I often want it on my schedule and in my way. Forgive me for my impatience, Lord. Teach me to rest in Your perfect timing.

Help me remember that You are never late, that You are always at work, and that Your love for my prodigal is greater than my own. When I am tempted to give up, renew my strength. When I demand answers, remind me that You see the whole story from beginning to end.

Keep my heart tender in the waiting. Do not let bitterness take root or despair have the final word. Use this season to make me more like Jesus—steadfast, prayerful, and full of faith. And when the day comes that my prodigal turns toward home, let me be ready to run with arms open wide.

In Jesus' name, Amen.

Affirmations

1. God's timing is never late and never wrong.

2. I will not rush what God is still preparing.

3. Waiting is not wasted; God is working in the unseen.

4. My prayers are not forgotten—they are being gathered by God.

5. I trust that God is writing a story greater than my plans.

6. I release control and rest in God's perfect pace.

7. What feels like delay may be divine protection.

8. I will stand in faith, not frustration, knowing His promises will come to pass.

9. Even when I don't understand the *when*, I will trust the *Who*.

10. God's plan for my prodigal—and for me—is unfolding right on time.

Prayer Focus

- Pray for strength to release control of your child or grandchild into God's hands.

- Ask God to teach you how to carry this burden *with* Him rather than on your own.

- Pray against guilt, shame, or false responsibility that weighs you down.

- Thank God daily that He carries both you and your prodigal in His loving arms.

A Letter of Eternal Hope

My Dear [Child's/Grandchild's Name],

Sometimes I carry the weight of worry for you so heavily it feels as though it might break me. I think about the choices you're making, the roads you're walking, and the risks that surround you. If I could, I would lift every burden from your shoulders and place it on mine.

But I've learned something important: God has already carried it. He took the heaviest weight at the cross and promises that His yoke is easy and His burden light. So instead of being crushed by fear, I choose to place both you and me into His hands.

I need you to know that you are not walking this journey alone. God is with you—whether you see Him or not. His love is stronger than your mistakes, deeper than your doubts, and greater than your struggles.

I will never stop carrying you in my prayers. But even more, I will rest in the truth that God Himself carries you every moment of your life.

Always love you. Always here for you.
[Your Name]

Chapter 3:
Praying with Authority and Boldness

When you love a prodigal, prayer can sometimes feel like a whisper into the wind. You pray, and nothing seems to change. You repeat the same requests, wondering if heaven has gone silent. At times, discouragement tempts you to stop altogether. But the truth is this: prayer is not weak, and it is never wasted. It is the most powerful weapon God has given you for your prodigal.

Scripture says, *"The prayer of a righteous person has great power as it is working"* (James 5:16). Prayer does not bounce off the ceiling—it moves the heart of God and wages war in the spiritual realm. We are not wrestling against flesh and blood but against unseen powers (Ephesians 6:12). When you pray, you are not begging for scraps; you are standing in authority as a child of the King, speaking His Word into your prodigal's life.

Think of Elijah, who prayed for rain after years of drought. At first, his servant saw nothing, but Elijah kept praying until a small cloud appeared (1 Kings 18:42–44). Your prayers may not seem to change things immediately, but they are shifting the unseen atmosphere. Every prayer plants a seed. Every declaration builds a foundation. Every intercession calls down God's kingdom into your child's life.

Praying with authority does not mean shouting louder or using special words. It means standing on God's promises with

15

confidence. It means praying Scripture, knowing His Word will not return void (Isaiah 55:11). It means asking in Jesus' name—not because you are worthy, but because He has given you His authority (John 14:13–14).

Your prodigal may resist your words, but they cannot resist your prayers. They may reject your advice, but they cannot escape the Spirit of God pursuing them through your intercession. You are not helpless; you are a warrior.

Practical Guidance

1. **Pray Scripture**
   Replace vague prayers with God's Word. Example: Instead of "God, help my child," pray, "Lord, bring them home like the prodigal son in Luke 15. Open their eyes as You did for the lost coin. Give them a new heart and a new spirit, as You promised in Ezekiel 36:26."

2. **Pray Out Loud**
   Speaking prayers audibly strengthens your faith and silences the enemy's lies. Declare truth over your home and your prodigal's life.

3. **Pray Daily**
   Set aside consistent times, even if brief. Prayer is not about length but persistence. Jesus told us to *"always pray and not lose heart"* (Luke 18:1).

4. **Fast with Prayer**
   Fasting sharpens spiritual authority (Matthew 17:21). Even a partial fast—giving up a meal, social media, or another comfort—can open spiritual breakthroughs.

5. **Form Prayer Partnerships**
   Share your burden with one or two trusted believers. When two agree in prayer, Jesus promises, *"It will be done"* (Matthew 18:19–20).

6. **Keep a Prayer Journal**
   Write your requests and record God's answers. Over time, you'll see His fingerprints, even in small ways, reminding you that He is always at work.

Prayer

Father,
I come before You, not in my own strength, but in the authority of Jesus' name. I lift my prodigal to You, declaring that they belong to You and not to the enemy. I speak life where there has been death, truth where there has been deception, and hope where there has been despair.

Lord, I declare Your Word over them: that You will remove their heart of stone and give them a heart of flesh (Ezekiel 36:26); that You will draw them with cords of lovingkindness (Jeremiah 31:3); that nothing can separate them from Your love (Romans 8:38–39).

I rebuke every chain of addiction, every lie of the enemy, every spirit of rebellion, in the name of Jesus. I release Your peace over their mind, Your healing over their wounds, and Your light into their darkness.

I will not give up, Lord. I will stand on Your promises, pray without ceasing, and believe for the day my prodigal comes home. Thank You that my prayers are powerful and effective because of Christ.

In Jesus' name, Amen.

Affirmations

1. My prayers are powerful because they rest on God's Word.
2. I do not beg—I declare promises as a child of the King.
3. The battle is not mine; it belongs to the Lord, who fights for my prodigal.

17

4. I will pray without ceasing and not lose heart.

5. God's Word spoken in prayer will not return void.

6. My prodigal cannot escape the reach of my prayers.

7. I have authority in Jesus' name to resist the enemy and speak life.

8. Every prayer I pray shifts the unseen spiritual battle.

9. I will persist like Elijah until I see God's cloud of mercy rising.

10. I am not helpless; I am a warrior in Christ.

Prayer Focus

- Pray for the Holy Spirit to guide your words so you pray according to God's will, not your fears.

- Ask God to increase your faith, even when circumstances seem unchanged.

- Declare specific Scriptures over your prodigal daily—reminding your heart and the enemy of God's promises.

- Thank God in advance for the breakthrough, trusting that He is already at work behind the scenes.

A Letter of Eternal Hope

My Dear [Child's/Grandchild's Name],

Every day, I lift your name before the throne of God. My prayers for you are not weak words whispered into the air—they are powerful because they are heard by the Almighty. He loves you more than I ever could, and He is working in ways I cannot see.

Sometimes it may seem as if nothing is changing, but I believe every prayer is like a seed planted in the soil of your life. In time, those seeds will grow into a harvest of faith, healing, and redemption. I trust that God is drawing you closer to Him, step by step.

No matter how far you wander, I will not stop praying. And no matter how long it takes, I will not lose hope. Your story isn't finished, and God's plans for you are good.

Always love you. Always here for you.
[Your Name]

Chapter 4:
Battling Shame, Blame, and Condemnation

Shame is a heavy cloak many parents and grandparents of prodigals wear. It whispers in your ear at night, follows you into church, and clings to you in family conversations. It tells you that you failed, that you're not good enough, that if you had done things differently, your prodigal would still be walking with God.

And sometimes it isn't just your own voice. Sometimes it's the words of others—spoken directly or implied in whispers. Family members who criticize your parenting. Friends who suggest their children turned out "right" because they did it better. Church members who silently judge, assuming they would have handled things differently. These words cut deeply because they land on an already tender heart.

But here is truth: shame and blame do not come from God. Romans 8:1 declares, *"There is therefore now no condemnation for those who are in Christ Jesus."* Condemnation is the voice of the enemy, not the voice of your Father.

Even the most faithful biblical figures knew the pain of rebellious children. Adam and Eve were directly created by God, yet one of their sons killed the other. David was a man after God's own heart, yet his children rebelled in devastating ways. If their families were not free from heartache, why should we expect ours

20

to be? Your prodigal's choices are not the measure of your worth as a parent or grandparent.

God does not shame you; He invites you into freedom. His voice does not condemn—it restores. He reminds you that you are loved, forgiven, and chosen. And He reminds you that while you influence your children, you are not their Savior. That role belongs to Him alone.

As for the voices of others, remember Paul's words: *"For am I now seeking the approval of man, or of God? If I were still trying to please man, I would not be a servant of Christ"* (Galatians 1:10). You do not answer to every critic. You answer to God, and He calls you beloved.

Practical Guidance

1. **Silence the Inner Accuser**
   When shame rises, confront it with Scripture. Say aloud: *"There is no condemnation for me in Christ"* (Romans 8:1).

2. **Respond (or Don't Respond) Wisely**
   Not every critic deserves a reply. Sometimes silence is your strength. If you must respond, keep it simple: "We're trusting God with our family."

3. **Surround Yourself with Safe People**
   Find friends or mentors who understand, who won't judge, and who will pray with you. Limit time with those who heap blame.

4. **Separate Your Identity from Your Prodigal's Choices**
   Their rebellion is not your identity. Your identity is in Christ—redeemed, chosen, and dearly loved.

5. **Turn Shame into Intercession**
   When criticism stings, use it as fuel for prayer. Instead of replaying the words, lay them before God and intercede for your prodigal.

21

6. **Seek Counseling if Needed**
   If shame has taken deep root, consider speaking with a Christian counselor who can help you process wounds and rebuild confidence in God's truth.

Prayer

Father,
I confess that I have carried shame like a heavy burden. I have blamed myself and listened to the voices of others who criticize and condemn. But today I choose to believe Your Word over every lie.

You say there is no condemnation for me because I am in Christ Jesus. You say that I am forgiven, chosen, and loved. Silence the voice of the enemy in my mind. Silence the whispers of guilt and failure. Teach me to walk in the freedom Jesus purchased for me.

Lord, when others judge me, help me not to grow bitter. Give me grace to forgive their words and courage to stand in truth. Help me live for Your approval, not the approval of people. Remind me that my prodigal's story is not over—and neither is mine.

I place all blame, shame, and judgment at the cross. I will not carry what Jesus has already carried for me. Fill me with peace, strength, and confidence in You.

In Jesus' name, Amen.

Affirmations

1. There is no condemnation for me in Christ Jesus (Romans 8:1).

2. My prodigal's choices do not define me; my identity is in Christ.

3. I am loved, forgiven, and chosen by God.

4. I will not live under the weight of shame.

5. I answer to God, not to human judgment.

6. Criticism will not break me; God's truth sustains me.

7. Shame is a lie, and I refuse to wear it any longer.

8. God has not abandoned me—He is with me in this season.

9. My story is not over, and neither is my prodigal's.

10. I walk in grace, freedom, and peace because of Jesus.

Prayer Focus

- Pray for freedom from the weight of shame and false guilt.

- Ask God to silence the enemy's lies and replace them with His truth.

- Declare that condemnation has no place in your heart or home—Christ has already paid it all.

- Thank God that He defines you and your prodigal not by mistakes, but by His love and redemption.

A Letter of Eternal Hope

My Dear [Child's/Grandchild's Name],

There have been times when I've carried shame because of your struggles. I've listened to whispers of blame—sometimes from others, sometimes from my own heart—that told me I should have done better or that I somehow failed you. But I know now those voices are not from God. His Word says there is no condemnation for those who belong to Christ Jesus.

You are not my shame. You are my beloved child, and more importantly, you are God's beloved. Nothing you've done can erase His love for you. Nothing you will do can make me stop loving you or praying for you.

I refuse to let shame or blame write our family's story. Instead, I believe in God's mercy and His power to turn every failure into testimony. Your life is not defined by mistakes—it is defined by grace.

Always love you. Always here for you.
[Your Name]

Chapter 5:
When You Feel Like Giving Up

There are moments in this journey when you feel you cannot go on. You've cried every tear, prayed every prayer, and given every ounce of energy you had. You've opened your door only to have it slammed in your face. You've offered help and been cursed for it. You've watched lie after lie, broken promise after broken promise, and your heart has been bruised again and again.

Maybe you've even said to yourself, *"I'm done. I can't take it anymore. I'm wiping my hands clean. They can live however they want, but I won't let it drag me down any further."*
If those words or thoughts have ever crossed your mind, you are not alone. Countless weary parents and grandparents have felt the same way.

Even Moses once told God, *"I am not able to carry all this people alone; the burden is too heavy for me"* (Numbers 11:14). Elijah, after great victories, collapsed under a tree and prayed that he might die, saying, *"It is enough; now, O Lord, take away my life"* (1 Kings 19:4). These were men of faith, and even they reached breaking points. God did not abandon them in their weakness—He met them with strength.

There is a difference between setting boundaries, which is necessary and wise, and giving up in despair. Boundaries protect you and your family; despair abandons hope altogether. God calls you to set boundaries with wisdom but never to abandon hope. Why?

25

Because He has not abandoned your prodigal. His love still pursues them. His Spirit still whispers. His mercy is still available.

Sometimes "stepping away" is actually the most faithful thing you can do. The father in Jesus' parable did not chase his son to the far country. He let him go, and it was there—in hunger and emptiness—that the son *"came to himself"* (Luke 15:17). There may be times when you must step back so your prodigal can face the full weight of their choices. That is not giving up; it is entrusting them into God's hands.

But when despair tempts you to quit praying, quit believing, or quit loving, remember this: God has not quit on you, and He has not quit on your prodigal. *"Let us not grow weary of doing good, for in due season we will reap, if we do not give up"* (Galatians 6:9).

Practical Guidance

1. **Differentiate Boundaries from Abandonment**
   Stepping back to protect your peace and family is not the same as cutting your prodigal off forever. Boundaries can be holy acts of love.

2. **Rest in God's Strength**
   Take time to recharge spiritually and physically. Like Elijah, sometimes you need to sleep, eat, and let God strengthen you before continuing.

3. **Shorten the Lens**
   Instead of focusing on *how long*, focus on *one day at a time*. Pray for strength for today, not answers for the next ten years.

4. **Find Support**
   Talk honestly with a trusted friend, pastor, or support group. Others can help carry the burden when you feel like setting it down.

26

5. **Surrender the Outcome Again**
   Every time you feel like walking away in despair, use it as a cue to place your prodigal back into God's hands. Whisper, *"Lord, they are Yours."*

6. **Celebrate Small Steps**
   Even if full restoration seems far away, thank God for small mercies—an answered text, a softened word, or a memory that sparks hope.

Prayer

Father,
I confess that I am weary. My strength is gone, my hope feels thin, and sometimes I want to wipe my hands clean and walk away. But You, Lord, are the God who never grows weary—the One who never gives up. I need Your strength in my weakness.

Help me to know when to step back with wisdom and when to keep pressing forward in love. Teach me the difference between setting healthy boundaries and giving up in despair. Protect my heart from bitterness. Fill me with Your Spirit so I will not quit praying, believing, and loving.

I release my prodigal into Your care again today. Where I can no longer reach, You still can. Where I have run out of words, Your Spirit still speaks. Remind me that the harvest comes "in due season" and that nothing is too hard for You.

Strengthen me, Lord, to keep going. Restore my hope, renew my faith, and carry me when I cannot walk on my own.

In Jesus' name, Amen.

Affirmations

1. I may be weary, but God renews my strength.

2. My prodigal's story is not finished.

27

3. I can set boundaries in love without giving up hope.

4. God has not abandoned me, and He has not abandoned my prodigal.

5. I will not quit praying; my prayers still matter.

6. The Lord is my strength when I have none of my own.

7. Giving up is not my story—endurance is.

8. In due season, I will see the fruit of my prayers.

9. What I cannot carry, God carries for me.

10. I will rest in God's timing and keep believing for redemption.

Prayer Focus

- Pray for endurance when discouragement tempts you to give up.

- Ask God to refresh your hope daily and remind you He is still working even when you cannot see it.

- Declare that your prayers are not wasted—every word has power and reaches heaven.

- Thank Him that He never grows weary and never stops pursuing your prodigal.

A Letter of Eternal Hope

My Dear [Child's/Grandchild's Name],

There have been moments when I've felt so tired, so worn down, that I wondered if I could keep praying for you. Waiting is hard, and sometimes it feels like nothing is changing. But every time I've felt close to giving up, God has reminded me of this truth: He has never once given up on you—and He never will.

You are worth every prayer. You are worth every tear. You are worth every long night of waiting and hoping. I believe with all my heart that God is writing a story of redemption for you, even now.

I will not stop. I will not give up. I will keep believing that your story isn't finished, and that the best is yet to come.

Always love you. Always here for you.
[Your Name]

Part II: The Hard Realities

The hardest part of loving a prodigal isn't always the distance; it's the storms you never saw coming. Addiction, broken relationships, danger, and despair can shake even the strongest heart. Yet in every hard reality, God remains near.

The chapters ahead will help you face truth with courage, set healthy boundaries, and hold tightly to the One who never lets go.

Chapter 6:
When Prodigals Are Addicted, Abusive, or Mentally Bound

Addiction has a way of swallowing everything in its path. It consumes trust, drains finances, shatters relationships, and replaces love with chaos. Whether it's alcohol, drugs, gambling, pornography, technology, or destructive relationships, addiction spreads like wildfire—consuming peace and leaving behind fear and brokenness. It is never just the addict who suffers; families carry the weight too.

Addiction isn't only physical—it is emotional, mental, and spiritual. Some prodigals are not enslaved to a substance but to patterns of thinking and feeling that keep them trapped. Fear, pride, shame, and bitterness can be prisons every bit as real as drugs or alcohol.

What It Means to Be Mentally Bound

Being mentally bound means being held captive by destructive thought patterns or emotional strongholds that shape how a person lives, reacts, and relates to others. The battle isn't merely physical—it takes place in the mind and spirit.

A mentally bound prodigal might:

- Be controlled by fear, anger, pride, or shame, distorting how they see God and others.

- Feel trapped in depression, anxiety, or trauma, unable to see hope clearly.

- Struggle with unforgiveness or bitterness that poisons relationships.

- Live in denial or self-deception, refusing to accept truth or responsibility.

- Be caught in emotional cycles—manipulation, control, self-hate—that keep them from healing.

The Bible calls these strongholds—patterns of thought that exalt themselves against the knowledge of God (2 Corinthians 10:4–5). Mental bondage is when lies replace truth, when a person believes things about themselves, others, or God that keep them in chains.

But the good news is this: Jesus came to set captives free—body, soul, and mind. Freedom begins when truth breaks through deception, when love overcomes fear, and when the mind is renewed by the Spirit of God (Romans 12:2).

And often, addiction is not silent. It brings storms of abuse—words spoken in rage, emotional manipulation, financial control, even physical harm. One day your prodigal may seem remorseful; the next, unpredictable and cruel. You may find yourself walking on eggshells, bracing for the next explosion, praying this time will be different.
Promises are made and broken again and again. *"I'll never do it again"* becomes a cycle that leaves you heartbroken and exhausted.

You love them deeply—yet you are also afraid. Afraid of what their choices mean for you, your spouse, your children, or your grandchildren. You wonder:

- *How do I love without enabling?*

- *How do I set boundaries without abandoning them?*

32

- *How do I protect my family when the person I love is also causing the harm?*

These are not easy questions, but Scripture does not ignore them. Proverbs teaches, *"The prudent sees danger and hides himself, but the simple go on and suffer for it"* (Proverbs 22:3). God calls you to love your prodigal—but He never calls you to be a victim of abuse or a participant in destruction. You were not created to be a verbal or physical target or a doormat. Love does not require surrendering your safety, sanity, or dignity.

Even the father in Jesus' parable set a boundary. He allowed his son to leave. He did not chase him into the far country, finance his rebellion, or protect him from consequences. He watched, waited, and prayed—but he did not compromise truth for comfort. It was the son's brokenness, not the father's intervention, that brought him home.

Love without wisdom becomes enabling; wisdom guided by love creates boundaries that protect life. Boundaries are not rejection—they are protection. They say, *"I love you, but I will not allow your choices to destroy what God has entrusted to me."*

Addiction and abuse thrive in secrecy, manipulation, and fear—but they lose power when exposed to light, truth, and accountability. The moment you bring them into God's light, you shift the battle from your hands to His.

Practical Guidance

1. **Protect Yourself and Those in Your Care**
    God calls you to love—but not to endure abuse. Emotional, verbal, or physical harm is never God's will for your life. If your prodigal is abusive, remove yourself and your loved ones from danger. Seek help if needed. Love does not equal tolerating violence; it means pursuing safety, truth, and healing.

33

2. **Set Clear, Prayerful Boundaries**
   Boundaries are not walls of rejection; they are lines of love drawn with wisdom. Decide what you will and will not allow: no money for destructive habits, no tolerance for manipulation, no compromise on safety. Stand firm. Your "no" may be the first "yes" to their recovery.

3. **Don't Try to Be Their Savior**
   You cannot fix or rescue your prodigal. That role belongs to Jesus alone. Let your love point them to Him, not to you. Rescue less, pray more, and release what only God can change.

4. **Expose the Darkness to the Light**
   Addiction and abuse thrive in secrecy. Don't hide the truth out of fear or shame. Speak with a trusted pastor, counselor, or support group. Bringing sin and suffering into the light is not betrayal—it is the beginning of freedom.

5. **Address Mental and Emotional Chains**
   Recognize that not all bondage is visible. If your prodigal struggles with depression, trauma, or mental illness, pray for clarity and compassion. Encourage professional help alongside prayer—God often heals through doctors, counselors, and community.

6. **Find Your Own Support**
   You cannot pour from an empty cup. Attend a Christian support group such as Celebrate Recovery, Al-Anon, or a church-based family ministry. Share your story with safe people who will pray for you, not judge you.

7. **Pray, Don't Preach**
   When emotions run high, silence can speak louder than words. Pray more than you argue. Bless them even when they push you away. God hears every whisper and can reach them in ways you never could.

8. **Allow Consequences to Teach**
   Sometimes love looks like stepping back. Allow your

prodigal to experience natural consequences. Pain often becomes the turning point God uses to break pride and open hearts.

9. **Guard Your Heart from Bitterness**
When betrayal or abuse runs deep, bitterness can grow quietly. Keep surrendering your pain to God. Forgiveness does not excuse what they've done—it frees you from being chained to their choices.

10. **Hold On to Hope**
Change rarely happens overnight. It often unfolds through surrender, failure, and grace. Keep praying. Keep believing. God specializes in impossible stories—and yours is not over.

Prayer

Father,
You see the pain addiction and brokenness have brought into our family. You see the confusion, the fear, and the exhaustion that come from loving someone trapped in bondage. I bring it all to You—the anger, the worry, the sleepless nights, and the ache that words cannot express.

You are the Healer of hearts and the Deliverer of souls. Break every chain of addiction, abuse, and mental bondage that holds my prodigal captive. Expose every lie they have believed and replace it with Your truth that sets them free. Restore clarity to their mind, tenderness to their heart, and purpose to their life.

Give me courage to love with wisdom—to say yes to what brings healing and no to what enables destruction. Help me set boundaries that protect, not out of anger, but out of obedience to Your Word. Fill my heart with compassion, yet keep me anchored in truth.

When I feel powerless, remind me You are still working. When I grow weary, be my strength. When hope feels distant, let Your promises speak louder than my fears. Teach me to trust You with my prodigal's story, especially the parts I cannot see.

Protect our family from the ripple effects of addiction and abuse. Surround us with Your peace. Guard our hearts from bitterness and our minds from despair. Cover our home in the blood of Jesus and drive out every spirit not from You.

Father, I release my prodigal into Your hands. I will no longer carry what only You can heal. I trust that You are pursuing them with a love that never quits and a grace that never runs dry.

In Jesus' mighty name, Amen.

Prayer Focus

- Pray for God to break every chain of addiction, abuse, and mental bondage.

- Ask the Holy Spirit to expose every lie your prodigal believes and replace it with truth.

- Pray for wisdom and courage to set godly boundaries that protect your home and peace.

- Ask God to surround your prodigal with divine appointments—voices of truth in their darkness.

- Pray for your own freedom from fear, guilt, and exhaustion, trusting God to restore your soul.

Affirmations

1. God is greater than any addiction or stronghold.
2. My love will not enable destruction; it will partner with God's truth.
3. I am called to peace, not chaos—to wisdom, not fear.
4. Setting boundaries is not rejection; it is obedience.

5. I refuse to live in secrecy or shame; I walk in light and truth.

6. God can heal what seems hopeless and redeem what looks ruined.

7. I will pray from faith, not fear.

8. The battle for my prodigal belongs to the Lord.

9. God protects, restores, and strengthens those who wait on Him.

10. Chains will break, minds will be renewed, and freedom will come—in God's time and God's way.

A Letter of Eternal Hope

My Dear [Child's/Grandchild's Name],

There are days when I look into your eyes and see both the person you were and the pain that holds you now. Addiction and anger have tried to steal the beautiful heart God placed inside you, but I know who you really are—and I will never stop believing for your freedom.

You may feel trapped by habits, fears, or voices that tell you you'll never change. But the truth is this: you are loved beyond measure by a God who still sets captives free. No chain is too thick for His mercy, no mind too clouded for His light. He has seen every battle you've fought, every tear you've cried, every promise you've made and broken—and still He calls you His.

I cannot fight your battles for you, but I can pray, and I do—every single day. I pray that you will come to the end of yourself and find the beginning of grace. I pray that the lies will lose their power and truth will rise within you like the dawn.

You are not forgotten. You are not forsaken. And even when you can't see the way home, God can.

Always love you. Always here for you.
[Your Name]

Chapter 7:
When Prodigals Disrupt the Family

Not every prodigal runs away. Some stay close. Some never leave at all. And sometimes the greatest heartbreak isn't found in distance—it's found in proximity. It's the tension of living under the same roof, sharing the same meals, and feeling your peace slowly unravel one outburst, one argument, one slammed door at a time.

When rebellion lives at home, it affects the entire household. The laughter grows quieter. The joy begins to fade. Everyone walks on eggshells, unsure which version of your prodigal will appear— the calm one who promises to do better or the one whose words slice through peace like a storm through glass.

You feel torn between compassion and exhaustion. Between wanting to help and needing to protect. Between loving your prodigal and fearing what their presence is doing to your marriage, your other children, or your grandchildren.

And then comes the guilt. You wonder, *"Am I a bad parent for needing space? Shouldn't I be able to love them through this?"* You sit in church and think, *"If they only knew what happens at home…"*

But hear this clearly: you are not a failure for having a prodigal under your roof. You are not weak for needing peace. You are not unloving for needing boundaries.

God never designed families to live in chaos. He designed homes to be sanctuaries—places of rest, laughter, and worship. The enemy loves to twist that design, bringing turmoil where there should be trust and disorder where there should be peace. Yet even in conflict, God's power to restore remains stronger than any disruption.

You may not be able to control your prodigal's choices, but you can choose what spirit rules your home. You can draw a line and declare, *"As for me and my house, we will serve the Lord"* (Joshua 24:15).

Your home still belongs to God. His peace still has authority there. And no matter how loud the chaos, His presence is greater.

When Love and Order Collide

You love your prodigal deeply, but their choices can unsettle everyone. Their moods shift the atmosphere, their words wound, and their habits drain emotional energy. You may feel torn between compassion and exhaustion, wondering, *"How do I love without losing my peace? How do I keep hope alive without allowing chaos to take root?"*

The answer isn't found in control—it's found in surrender. You cannot force your prodigal to change, but you can decide what spirit will rule your home. As Joshua declared, *"As for me and my house, we will serve the Lord"* (Joshua 24:15).

That declaration is not just a plaque on a wall; it is a line drawn in the sand. It says: *"This home belongs to God. Fear, anger, and division have no place here."*

You are not rejecting your prodigal by setting boundaries; you are protecting what God has entrusted to you. Boundaries are love in structure. They say, *"I care too much to let sin destroy this space."*

Protecting the Family

When a prodigal disrupts the peace of your home, balance compassion with wisdom:

- **Guard your atmosphere.** Begin each morning with prayer and worship. Invite God to fill your home before conflict begins.

- **Stay united as caregivers.** The enemy loves to divide. Talk, pray, and decide together how to respond.

- **Protect the vulnerable.** Shield children and grandchildren from unhealthy behavior or toxic speech. Their hearts need safety and stability.

- **Don't let fear guide your responses.** Fear tells you to tiptoe for the sake of peace, but real peace comes from truth spoken in love.

Romans 12:18 says, *"If possible, so far as it depends on you, live peaceably with all."* Sometimes peace requires distance. Sometimes it requires firm boundaries. Always, it requires surrender to the Holy Spirit.

Declaring Peace Over Your Home

Jesus said, "Peace I leave with you; my peace I give to you" (John 14:27).

That promise is meant for your household. You have the authority to declare that peace daily:

- "Lord, let Your peace fill this home."

- "Drive out every spirit of fear, conflict, and confusion."

- "Establish Your presence in every room, every heart, every conversation."

Peace is not the absence of trouble; it is the presence of Jesus in the middle of it.

Scripture Anchors

- *"The prudent sees danger and hides himself..."* — Proverbs 22:3

- *"If possible, so far as it depends on you, live peaceably with all."* — Romans 12:18

- *"Peace I leave with you; my peace I give to you."* — John 14:27

- *"No weapon...shall succeed."* — Isaiah 54:17

- *"As for me and my house, we will serve the Lord."* — Joshua 24:15

Practical Guidance

1. **Claim Spiritual Authority Over Your Home**
   Pray out loud, anoint doorways, and declare that your household belongs to Jesus. His peace is stronger than any chaos.

2. **Set Clear Household Expectations**
   You can love your prodigal and still require respect. Clarify that destructive behavior—anger, manipulation, or substance use—will not be tolerated.

3. **Stay Spiritually and Emotionally Connected**
   Keep communication open among family members. Don't let one person's rebellion divide the rest.

4. **Protect Children and Grandchildren**
   Shield them from outbursts or manipulation. Teach them that love and boundaries can coexist.

5. **Don't Hide the Problem**
   Reach out to trusted Christian friends, mentors, or counselors. Healing begins with honesty, not secrecy.

6. **Invite God's Presence Daily**
   Read Scripture aloud. Play worship music. Let God's Word shape the atmosphere.

7. **Know When Space Is Necessary**
   If the home becomes unsafe, it is not unloving to ask your prodigal to leave. Some restoration requires distance.

8. **Refuse to Live in Shame**
   You are not defined by your prodigal's behavior. God honors your desire to build a home of faith.

9. **Guard Against Division and Despair**
   The enemy attacks unity. Keep praying, keep forgiving, and keep hope alive.

10. **Speak God's Promises Over Your Home**
    Your words create atmosphere. Declare peace, faith, and life each day.

Prayer

Lord,
You see the turmoil that fills our home. You know the tension, the hurt, and the fear that linger in the air. Yet You are still the Prince of Peace. Today, I declare that this home belongs to You.

Let Your presence drive out every spirit of strife. Fill these rooms with Your light. Replace every harsh word with grace and every anxious thought with calm.

Give us courage to speak truth with love and wisdom to set healthy boundaries. Protect the innocent, heal the wounded, and reach the one who is running.

Bring peace where there has been chaos, unity where there has been division, and love where there has been fear.

In the powerful name of Jesus, Amen.

Affirmations

1. My home belongs to the Lord, and His peace rules here.

2. Fear has no permanent place in my household.

3. I can set healthy boundaries and still love my prodigal.

4. God's wisdom gives me courage to make hard choices.

5. The enemy's chaos cannot overtake Christ's peace.

6. My family is covered by the blood of Jesus.

7. I refuse to live in shame; I will live in truth.

8. No weapon formed against my family will prosper.

9. Where the Spirit of the Lord is, there is freedom—even here.

10. God is restoring peace and order to our home one day at a time.

Prayer Focus

- Pray for genuine peace—not passive quiet, but the presence of God.

- Ask God to heal strained relationships within your home.

- Pray for unity and discernment among parents, grandparents, or caregivers.

- Thank God that He is Lord over your household and no scheme of the enemy can overturn His work.

A Letter of Eternal Hope

My Dear [Child's/Grandchild's Name],

There have been moments when your choices brought tension into our home, and those moments have been painful. But I want you to know this: my love for you has not changed. And God's love for you has never wavered.

You may not realize how deeply your actions affect those who care for you, but I still believe that one day you will see the beauty of restoration God can bring. I pray that peace will fill your heart, just as God fills our home again with His grace.

You are not forgotten, and you are not forsaken. The same God who calmed storms at sea can calm the storms within us—and I believe He will.

Always love you. Always here for you.
[Your Name]

Chapter 8:
When Prodigals Make Life-Altering Choices

Some choices are not small detours; they are collisions that leave lasting damage. A prodigal may become pregnant or father a child before they are ready. They may commit a crime that leads to jail time. They may marry unwisely, divorce painfully, or abandon their children. They may walk away from school or career, plunge into financial ruin, or entangle themselves in relationships that tear the family apart.

As a parent or grandparent, these moments can feel like standing on the shore, watching your child sail straight into a storm. You see the danger. You know the pain that lies ahead. You call out warnings, but your words are ignored. The helplessness is overwhelming.

In those moments, you wonder, *What will this mean for their future? What about their children? What about us?* Shame creeps in, whispering that their choices expose your failures. Anger rises at wasted potential. Grief overtakes you as innocent lives—siblings, grandchildren, or spouses—are pulled into the fallout. Exhaustion sets in from constantly trying to pick up the pieces of someone else's decisions.

The Bible is honest about choices that carry lasting consequences. Esau sold his birthright for a single meal and could not reverse the decision (Genesis 25; Hebrews 12:16–17). Samson revealed his secret to Delilah, lost his strength, and became a prisoner (Judges 16). David sinned with Bathsheba, and though God

45

forgave him, his family bore the scars for generations (2 Samuel 12). The prodigal son wasted his inheritance in reckless living, and the money was never restored (Luke 15:13).

Yet in every one of these stories, God's mercy still shines. Esau was still blessed. Samson's strength returned in his final hour. David was restored as a man after God's own heart. Peter, who denied Jesus three times, was reinstated and became a leader of the early church. The prodigal son, though bankrupt, was welcomed home with compassion. Wrong choices leave scars, but God can use even scars to tell a story of redemption.

For families, the fallout of life-altering choices is heavy. Unexpected pregnancies or fatherhood may bring the responsibility of caring for a child in unstable conditions. Legal trouble may lead to court hearings, bail money, jail visits, and criminal records that follow for years. Financial collapse may bring drained bank accounts, debt, eviction, or lost jobs. Relationships may fracture through divorce, domestic violence, or toxic partnerships. The generational impact can be devastating—grandchildren born into chaos, siblings traumatized, reputations damaged. These consequences are real and cannot always be erased. But they can be redeemed.

In these seasons, you must face reality honestly. Denial delays healing. God invites you to bring the truth into His presence and admit, *"Lord, this is painful and costly, but You are still sovereign."* Allow consequences to speak when they must. Shielding your prodigal from fallout may rob them of the lessons they most need to learn. Pain often teaches what pride refuses to hear.

Yet love does not disappear in the midst of hard truth. You can love without endorsing, telling your prodigal, *"I will always love you, but I cannot support this decision."* Compassion and boundaries can stand side by side.

It is also essential to protect the innocent. When grandchildren, spouses, or others are affected, they need safety and stability. This may mean stepping in with guardianship, childcare, or consistent emotional support. At the same time, you must establish financial boundaries. Draining your retirement, covering endless bail, or funding destructive habits will not heal your prodigal. Instead, direct your resources toward redemptive support: rehab, counseling, childcare, or ministry—not rebellion.

When the fallout feels overwhelming, seek help from those equipped to walk alongside you. Lawyers, counselors, social workers, and church ministries may all be part of God's provision. You do not have to carry this alone. Most of all, pray not only for reversal but for redemption. Some decisions cannot be undone, but God can redeem even irreversible consequences. Romans 8:28 promises that He works all things together for good, and Isaiah 61:3 declares that He gives beauty for ashes. Redemption may not erase scars, but it can make them shine with grace.

Through it all, guard your own heart against bitterness. The longer consequences last, the greater the temptation to harden. If you hand your pain to God each day, He will keep your hope alive. Bitterness poisons, but hope sustains. Your prodigal's story is not finished—and neither is yours. God is still writing.

Practical Guidance

1. **Acknowledge Reality**
   Do not pretend the choice is minor. Face it honestly before God: *"Lord, this decision hurts, but I give it to You."*

2. **Allow Consequences to Teach**
   Shielding your prodigal from the results of their decisions may prolong their rebellion. Sometimes pain becomes the teacher that pride resists.

3. **Love Without Endorsing**
   You can say, *"I love you, but I cannot support this choice."* This protects relationship without compromising truth.

47

4. **Support the Innocent**
   If children or others are harmed by your prodigal's choices, step in with love and stability for those who cannot protect themselves.

5. **Pray for Redemption, Not Just Reversal**
   Some choices cannot be undone—but God can still redeem them. Pray for His mercy to bring beauty from ashes (Isaiah 61:3).

6. **Guard Against Bitterness**
   Long-term consequences can tempt you toward anger or cynicism. Lay your burdens before the Lord daily so bitterness does not poison your heart.

Scriptures

- *"For I know the plans I have for you... to give you a future and a hope."* — Jeremiah 29:11

- *"We know that for those who love God all things work together for good."* — Romans 8:28

- *"...to bestow on them a crown of beauty instead of ashes."* — Isaiah 61:3

- *"Restore to me the joy of your salvation."* — Psalm 51:12

Prayer

Father,
You see the choices my prodigal has made—choices that grieve my heart and carry lasting consequences. I confess that I wish I could undo them, but I know only You can redeem them.

Give me courage to stand in truth without compromise and to love without enabling. Show me how to offer grace while still protecting my family. If innocent lives are affected, help me step in with compassion and wisdom.

Lord, I place every decision, every mistake, every consequence into Your hands. I believe that what the enemy meant for harm, You can use for good. Bring beauty from ashes, healing from brokenness, and redemption from rebellion.

Restore hope to my heart, Lord. Remind me that no decision is too great for Your mercy to cover. I entrust the future of my prodigal into Your hands, knowing You are the God of new beginnings.

In Jesus' name, Amen.

Affirmations

1. No decision is too big for God to redeem.

2. My prodigal's mistakes do not cancel God's promises.

3. I can love without condoning destructive choices.

4. Consequences may teach what my words cannot.

5. God's mercy is greater than my prodigal's failure.

6. I will not grow bitter; I will stay rooted in hope.

7. What the enemy meant for harm, God can use for good.

8. My prayers invite redemption into irreversible situations.

9. The future is in God's hands, not locked in the prodigal's past.

10. I believe beauty can rise from ashes.

Prayer Focus

- Pray for God to protect your prodigal from irreversible harm even in their poor decisions.

- Ask for divine intervention where their choices could alter their future—jobs, relationships, finances, health.

- Pray for wisdom to know when to step in and when to step back, trusting God's timing.

- Thank Him that even when choices carry consequences, His mercy can reshape the ending.

A Letter of Eternal Hope

My Dear [Child's/Grandchild's Name],

Some of the choices you've made have left me fearful and heartbroken. I've worried about where those decisions might lead you, and at times it has felt like watching someone walk toward a cliff. But even in the face of consequences, my love for you is unshaken.

I want you to know this: no decision you make can ever put you beyond God's reach. Even when you take paths that bring pain or regret, He is still the God who redeems, restores, and makes all things new.

I may not be able to protect you from every outcome, but I will keep praying for you and believing in the One who holds your future. I believe that one day you will look back and see how God took even the hardest choices and used them to draw you closer to Him.

Always love you. Always here for you.
[Your Name]

Chapter 9:
When Prodigals Don't See Their Need for God

Some prodigals don't simply wander from God—they reject Him outright. They feel angry about what life has dealt them and blame everyone else for their pain. They create their own definition of "truth" to justify their choices. They convince themselves they don't need God, prayer, or salvation.

What makes this so painful is that they may not even recognize that their life is broken. They don't see the damage in their relationships, their habits, or their future. In their mind, it is always someone else's fault—the parent who raised them, the friend who betrayed them, the church that disappointed them, the God they say has failed them. Blindness covers their eyes and pride hardens their heart.

This is not a new story. Pharaoh hardened his heart repeatedly even as Egypt collapsed around him. The Pharisees stood face to face with Jesus yet refused to acknowledge their need. Saul persecuted believers violently until one encounter with Christ changed everything. Scripture shows us that unbelief, pride, and anger can grip the heart—but none of them are stronger than the mercy of God.

So when your prodigal says they don't need God, do not believe the lie that their story is finished. God is not threatened by their denial. He is not shaken by their anger. He remains patient, persistent, and faithful to seek and save the lost—even those who do not know they are lost.

Scriptures to Declare

- *"The god of this world has blinded the minds of the unbelievers, to keep them from seeing the light of the gospel."* — 2 Corinthians 4:4

- *"I will give you a new heart and put a new spirit within you. I will remove the heart of stone and give you a heart of flesh."* — Ezekiel 36:26

- *"For the Son of Man came to seek and to save the lost."* — Luke 19:10

- *"Saul, Saul, why are you persecuting me? ... And immediately something like scales fell from his eyes."* — Acts 9:4, 18

- *"The Lord is not slow to fulfill his promise... but is patient toward you, not wishing that any should perish."* — 2 Peter 3:9

Practical Guidance

1. **Don't Argue with Blindness**
   When your prodigal refuses to see their need for God, remember that you cannot reason someone out of spiritual blindness. Only the Holy Spirit can open the eyes of the heart. Arguments rarely lead to repentance; prayer and love often do. Instead of debates, speak peace and stand firm in quiet faith. The God who opened Saul's eyes can open theirs as well—often when you are not even present.

2. **Keep Reflecting God's Character**
   When your prodigal misrepresents who God is—calling Him unfair, harsh, or distant—let your life show them something different. Be gracious when they expect condemnation, patient when they expect anger, and kind when they expect rejection. Your life may become the clearest picture of God they ever see.

3. **Pray Against Pride and Deception**
   Pride blinds, and deception binds. Ask God to uproot every false belief that says, "I don't need Him," or "I can manage on my own." Pray for moments of clarity that break through arrogance and awaken conviction without shame.

4. **Release the Illusion of Control**
   You cannot save your prodigal or make them see their need. Salvation belongs to the Lord. When you release your desire to control and shift the battle to prayer, you place them in God's hands—the safest place they could be.

5. **Love Without Preaching**
   A hardened heart often ignores spiritual lectures but watches behavior closely. Love them without striving. Listen more than you correct. Show calm when they are hostile. Sometimes love becomes the sermon that softens the soil of their heart.

6. **Guard Your Own Faith**
   Hearing someone you love reject God can wear down the spirit. Don't let their unbelief weaken your hope. Stay anchored in Scripture and close to believers who remind you that God is still working even when you cannot see evidence.

7. **Pray for Divine Encounters**
   Ask God to meet them in ways you cannot—through dreams, conversations, unexpected circumstances, or a sense of emptiness that brings them to truth. God is not limited to sermons or church walls. He knows how to find the wandering.

8. **Be Ready When Their Eyes Open**
   One day, the questions will come. Pride will crack. Desperation will whisper. When that moment arrives, meet them with grace, not judgment. Be the reflection of the

Father who ran to meet the prodigal while he was still far off.

9. **Stand Firm in Hope**
   When nothing seems to change, remember that God's timing is different from yours. His patience is mercy at work. Every prayer, every tear, and every moment of waiting moves the story toward redemption. Even when your prodigal says, "I don't need God," God is still saying, "I want you."

Prayer

Father,

I bring before You my prodigal—the one who insists they don't need You and says they are fine on their own. They don't see the cracks in their heart or the emptiness in their soul, but You see what they cannot. You know what lies beneath the pride and the anger.

Do what only You can do. Break through the darkness that blinds their eyes. Tear down the walls pride has built. Replace every false image of You with the truth of Your mercy and grace.

Where their heart is hardened, soften it. Where conviction has been silenced, awaken it. Where excuses are built, dismantle them gently with truth. Let the emptiness of life without You become so unbearable that they finally turn toward the light.

Forgive me for trying to force what only Your Spirit can accomplish. Help me to love with patience, pray with faith, and trust with confidence. Remind me that You are not intimidated by their denial or rebellion. You are patient and relentless in love.

Open their eyes as You opened Saul's. Let the scales fall. Let Your light break through. And when that moment comes, let them find You waiting with open arms, ready to redeem what once seemed lost.

Until that day, I will keep praying, believing, and loving—because I know their story is not over.

In Jesus' name, Amen.

Affirmations

1. My prodigal's blindness cannot outlast God's light.

2. Their anger cannot drive God away.

3. God's truth will expose every lie.

4. A hardened heart can soften again.

5. Pride is no match for God's mercy.

6. God's patience is unstoppable love in action.

7. Even when they reject Him, God still pursues them.

8. The God who opened Saul's eyes can open theirs.

9. Their unbelief cannot cancel God's plan.

10. Their story is still being written by God.

Prayer Focus

- **Pray for spiritual eyes to open.** Ask God to lift the veil that blinds your prodigal to truth.

- **Pray for a softened heart.** Ask the Lord to replace their heart of stone with a heart of flesh.

- **Pray for divine encounters.** Ask God to meet them through circumstances, people, or moments that awaken truth.

- **Pray for truth to replace deception.** Ask God's Word to cut through confusion and lies.

- **Pray for patience in your own heart.** Ask God to keep your hope alive while you wait.

- **Declare over your prodigal:** *"You will see God as He truly is. Your heart will turn. Your eyes will open. Your life will be redeemed by His grace."*

A Letter of Eternal Hope

My Dear [Child's/Grandchild's Name],

I know you don't think you need God. I've heard your words and felt the weight of your anger. I know you've blamed Him, and at times blamed others, for the pain you've carried. You believe you can face life on your own.

But I want you to know this: God is not offended by your questions. He is not shaken by your anger. And He has not stopped loving you—not for one moment. He sees the hurt you won't admit and the cracks you try to hide. And still, He calls you His.

You may not see it now, but the same God you resist has been pursuing you all along. His love is not fragile. It is steady, relentless, and patient beyond understanding. You can ignore Him or run from Him, but you cannot outrun His grace. One day, I believe the scales will fall from your eyes, and you will see Him as He truly is—the One who has been running toward you all this time.

Until that day, I will keep praying and believing. Your story is not finished, and God has not stopped writing it. You are never too far, never too lost, never too proud for His love to reach you.

Always love you. Always here for you.
[Your Name]

Chapter 10:
Communicating with Prodigals

Few things feel more fragile than conversations with a prodigal. Words meant to express love may be twisted into accusations. Efforts to speak truth may be dismissed as lectures. A simple question about their well-being may stir defensiveness or anger. Parents and grandparents often feel as if they are walking on eggshells, afraid the wrong word will push their prodigal even farther away.

The tension is real. Silence can feel like neglect, yet speaking can feel like risk. The enemy uses this tension to create fear, confusion, and distance. But God gives wisdom for our words. Scripture says, "Let your speech always be gracious, seasoned with salt, so that you may know how you ought to answer each person" (Colossians 4:6). It also reminds us that "a soft answer turns away wrath, but a harsh word stirs up anger" (Proverbs 15:1). Communication with prodigals requires balance under the guidance of the Holy Spirit, combining grace with truth, listening with speaking, and patience with conviction.

Jesus modeled this balance perfectly. He listened with compassion, asked heart-searching questions, and spoke truth in love. With the Samaritan woman, He began with a simple request for water before gently revealing her need for living water (John 4). With Peter after his denial, He did not lecture. Instead, He asked three restoring questions: "Do you love Me?" (John 21:15–17). Jesus shows us that communication with prodigals is less about winning arguments and more about opening doors for the Holy Spirit to work.

57

There is also a crucial truth: communication must never come at the cost of safety. If a conversation becomes abusive, manipulative, or dangerous, you have the God-given right to step away. Proverbs 22:3 says, "The prudent sees danger and hides himself, but the simple go on and suffer for it." Allowing yourself to be cursed at, belittled, threatened, or intimidated does not prove love. It endangers your heart and dishonors the peace God intends for your home. Healthy communication requires healthy boundaries. You may say, "I love you, but I will not stay in a conversation where I am being abused." Walking away from destructive dialogue is not rejection. It is wisdom.

Practical Guidance

1. **Listen before you speak.**
   Your prodigal may expect judgment, so surprise them with patience. Listening does not mean agreement; it simply acknowledges their value as a person and opens space for honest dialogue.

2. **Choose your words intentionally.**
   Avoid lectures, angry ultimatums, or constant reminders of failure. Ask reflective questions instead: "How are you really doing?" or "What do you hope for in the future?" These invite conversation rather than closing it.

3. **Be mindful of timing.**
   Difficult conversations rarely go well in heated moments. Pray for Spirit-led opportunities. The right words at the wrong time can cause harm. Trust God to open doors, and be ready when they appear.

4. **Keep truth and love together.**
   Affirm your love while refusing to support destructive choices. Say, "I love you deeply. Because I love you, I cannot support this path, but nothing will make me stop caring for you." Truth spoken gently carries weight.

5. **Protect yourself and your home.**
   If a prodigal becomes verbally cruel, manipulative, or violent, step away. Hang up the phone, leave the room, or decline the conversation. If safety is at risk, call for help. Communication that empowers abuse is not biblical love. God calls you to love, but He also calls you to guard the peace He entrusted to you.

Prayer

Father,
You know how fragile my words feel with my prodigal. I want to speak life, yet I fear saying too much or too little. Give me wisdom. Season my speech with grace. Teach me to listen first, to wait on Your timing, and to speak only what builds up.

Protect me from fear-driven conversations. Guard me from anger, manipulation, or despair. Give me courage to walk away from words that wound and to set boundaries where abuse arises. Help me reflect Jesus in patience, gentleness, and truth.

Let my prodigal hear not only my voice, but Your love behind every word. And when silence is better than speech, let my prayers stand in the gap. Use every conversation and every moment of restraint for Your glory.

In Jesus' name, Amen.

Affirmations

1. My words carry life when surrendered to God.

2. I do not need the perfect phrase; the Holy Spirit gives wisdom.

3. I can speak truth in love without fear.

4. Listening is as powerful as speaking.

5. God can speak where my words cannot reach.

6. Silence, prayer, and patience are also expressions of love.

7. I will not give up on communicating with my prodigal.

8. My love can be expressed even in simple, sincere words.

9. God is the ultimate communicator, and His voice is stronger than mine.

10. Every word of grace is a seed God can use.

Prayer Focus

- Pray for wisdom to know when to speak and when to remain silent.

- Ask God to make your words gentle, firm, and filled with grace.

- Pray that your prodigal will hear love, not judgment, behind every word.

- Thank God that His Spirit speaks to them in ways beyond your reach.

A Letter of Eternal Hope

My Dear [Child's/Grandchild's Name],

I know there are times when our conversations do not go the way either of us desires. Words get misunderstood, emotions rise, and silence settles between us. But I want you to know this: every word I speak to you comes from love.

Even when my words are imperfect, even when we fail to understand one another, I hope you can still hear my heart. I am for you. I believe in you. And more than anything, I love you.

No wall of silence is too high for God to break down. No harsh word is beyond His healing. I believe the day will come when our conversations are filled with peace, understanding, and hope again. Until then, I will keep praying for wisdom, patience, and the right words at the right time.

Always love you. Always here for you.
[Your Name]

Chapter 11:
When Prodigals Threaten to Harm Themselves or Others

Few situations create more fear than realizing your child or grandchild may harm themselves, hurt someone else, or destroy what surrounds them. This is not ordinary rebellion. It is crisis. It is the moment when fear and faith collide, when your prayers become desperate cries for divine intervention, and when you feel helpless watching a spiritual storm you cannot stop.

Sometimes a prodigal's pain turns inward through self-harm, reckless behavior, dangerous addictions, or suicidal thoughts. At other times, it turns outward through explosive anger, threats, or violence that leaves your home shaken. What you see is only the surface of something far deeper: torment, shame, confusion, and a desperate search for relief.

When your prodigal enters this kind of darkness, you feel torn between protecting them and protecting everyone else. You want to believe they will calm down. You want to believe your love is enough. Yet there comes a moment when the danger can no longer be ignored. This is not the time to hope it will get better on its own. It is the time to act, pray, and protect.

You may feel guilty for admitting the danger. You may fear that calling for help will make matters worse. But hear this clearly: God does not call you to silence in a storm. He calls you to wisdom and courage. Love does not mean allowing destruction. Love means stepping into the fire with prayer and protection.

Proverbs 27:12 teaches, "The prudent sees danger and takes refuge." Faith and action must work together. Calling for help is not failure. It is obedience to God's call to preserve life.

Even in crisis, God is present. He was with Elijah under the broom tree when the prophet begged to die. He was with the man in the tombs who tore himself apart until Jesus restored him. He was with the disciples when the storm threatened to sink their boat. In every story, God intervened—not too early, not too late, but right on time.

Practical Guidance

1. **Call for help immediately.**
   If your prodigal threatens to harm themselves or others, or destroys property in rage, contact emergency services or go directly to a hospital. This is not a lack of faith. It is partnership with God's protection. You can pray and protect at the same time.

2. **Do not handle it alone.**
   If you feel unsafe, do not confront them by yourself. Reach out to a trusted friend, a pastor, a counselor, or a trained crisis responder. Two are stronger than one (Ecclesiastes 4:12). God never intended you to carry this alone.

3. **Secure the environment.**
   Remove or hide weapons, alcohol, drugs, or objects that could cause harm. Keep car keys, medications, or valuables out of reach. Create a safe zone in your home—physically and emotionally.

4. **Stay calm when the atmosphere is charged.**
   Rage grows when met with reaction. Lower your voice. Slow your breathing. Speak peace even when your heart is racing. Say what matters most: "I love you. You are not

alone. Help is coming." Your calmness becomes a lifeline in chaos.

5. **Listen beneath the anger.**
   Anger often hides pain. After the immediate crisis passes, gently ask questions such as, "What is hurting you right now?" For many prodigals, fury is a mask for fear.

6. **Seek professional and spiritual support.**
   After the crisis, involve both mental-health professionals and spiritual mentors. Healing rarely happens instantly, but it begins when truth is acknowledged and help is accepted.

7. **Protect the innocent.**
   If children, spouses, or elderly family members are exposed to danger, protect them first. Remove them from harm's reach. God never asks you to sacrifice the safety of one soul to save another.

8. **Guard your own heart.**
   Crisis leaves wounds. Seek support through counseling, pastoral care, or a prayer group. Even Jesus withdrew to quiet places to restore His strength (Luke 5:16).

9. **Document and prepare.**
   If the danger returns, keep notes of incidents, dates, and any threats. This becomes essential if professional or legal intervention is needed. Planning ahead is not fear. It is stewardship.

10. **Invite God's presence into the chaos.**
    Read Psalm 91 aloud in your home. Declare His promises. Pray:
    "Lord, fill this place with Your peace. Drive out fear, anger, and darkness in Jesus' name."

Scriptures to Declare

- *"The Lord is near to the brokenhearted and saves the crushed in spirit."* — Psalm 34:18

- *"When you pass through the waters, I will be with you."* — Isaiah 43:2

- *"He will command His angels concerning you to guard you in all your ways."* — Psalm 91:11

- *"The Lord will fight for you; you need only to be still."* — Exodus 14:14

- *"The name of the Lord is a strong tower; the righteous run into it and are safe."* — Proverbs 18:10

Prayer

Father,
I come to You in distress. I see danger surrounding my prodigal— sometimes in their words, sometimes in their eyes, and sometimes in their actions. Fear grips me, yet I know You are stronger than the darkness that hunts them.

Protect them from harm, both from others and from themselves. Surround them with Your angels. Calm the storm inside their mind. Bring clarity where there is confusion, and peace where there is rage.

Give me wisdom to know when to act, when to speak, and when to stay silent. Help me protect my home, my family, and my own heart without shame or guilt.

When I cannot reach them, reach them Yourself. Step into the chaos, interrupt their destruction, and rescue them with Your power. No pit is too deep and no heart too broken for Your saving hand.

In Jesus' name, Amen.

Affirmations

1. I can love my prodigal and still set boundaries.

2. God is my protector and refuge in every storm.

3. My prodigal's life is in God's hands, not mine.

4. I will not let fear silence my wisdom or my prayers.

5. Seeking help is not failure; it is faith in action.

6. God's angels guard our family day and night.

7. The enemy will not destroy what God intends to redeem.

8. Hope is not lost; healing is still possible.

9. I can trust God's plan even in chaos.

10. The light of Christ shines in the darkest places.

Prayer Focus

- Pray for God's protection over your prodigal and all who are near them.

- Ask the Holy Spirit to reveal any hidden pain or trauma fueling their rage or despair.

- Pray for discernment to know when to act and when to step back.

- Pray for emergency responders, counselors, and ministries that serve struggling families.

- Thank God in advance for preserving life and rewriting the story with mercy.

A Letter of Eternal Hope

My Dear [Child's/Grandchild's Name],

I have seen you when the darkness feels overwhelming, when anger or despair seems to take over. I know there are moments when you cannot see a way out or when you feel ready to strike against everything around you. Even in those moments, you are not beyond God's reach.

No matter what you have done, or how deep the pain goes, God still loves you. He sees your struggle. He has not turned away. He is still fighting for you.

If you ever feel lost or alone, remember this: you do not have to face it by yourself. I am praying for you. I am believing for you. And the God who created you still has a plan for your life—a plan filled with hope and a future.

Always love you. Always here for you.
[Your Name]

Chapter 12:
Facing Public Shame and Judgment

When you love a prodigal, the pain is not only private. Often it becomes public. Friends, extended family, neighbors, or church members may notice your prodigal's absence, hear rumors about their behavior, or witness their rebellion firsthand. You may feel the sting of whispers, the weight of sideways glances, or the ache of silence when others don't know what to say. At times, people even speak directly, offering comments that wound: "If that were my child, I would never let that happen." "Where did you go wrong?" "You should have done it differently."

Shame grows in these moments. You find yourself dreading social gatherings, avoiding questions, or hiding the truth because explaining it feels too painful. Judgment—whether imagined or real—becomes another layer of suffering on top of the grief you already carry. The enemy uses this to isolate you, whispering lies that you are alone, unworthy, or responsible for every choice your prodigal has made.

But God's Word reminds us that we live for His approval, not the opinions of others. Paul wrote, "For am I now seeking the approval of man, or of God? If I were still trying to please man, I would not be a servant of Christ" (Galatians 1:10). Even Jesus was misunderstood, criticized, and condemned by the religious leaders of His day. If the perfect Son of God faced public judgment, it is no surprise when we experience it as well.

You are not defined by the whispers of others. You are defined by the voice of God. Shame says you are a failure. Condemnation says you are not enough. But the Father says you are His beloved child, chosen and redeemed. As Isaiah 54:4 promises, "Fear not, for you will not be ashamed; be not confounded, for you will not be disgraced."

Practical Guidance

1. **Anchor your identity in Christ.**
   Remind yourself daily: "I am not defined by my prodigal's choices. I am defined by Christ's love."

2. **Respond with grace, or choose silence.**
   Not every critic deserves a reply. If you do respond, keep it simple: "We are trusting God with our family."

3. **Choose safe circles.**
   Surround yourself with people who pray for you, not those who gossip about you. Limit time with anyone who only criticizes.

4. **Release the need to explain.**
   You do not owe everyone the details of your story. Share only with trusted friends or mentors who can carry it with compassion.

5. **Turn shame into prayer.**
   Each time you feel embarrassed or judged, whisper, "Lord, this is Yours. Cover me in Your peace."

6. **Remember you are not alone.**
   Many faithful parents and grandparents have walked this path. Elijah felt alone, but God showed him thousands who remained faithful (1 Kings 19:18).

7. **Keep serving and living.**
   Do not let shame push you out of community. Stay

69

engaged in worship, service, and fellowship. Your story may encourage someone more than you know.

Prayer

Father,
You know the sting of words spoken against me and the weight of whispers behind my back. You know the heaviness I feel when others judge my family or assume they understand our story. I confess that shame has tried to silence me, yet today I choose to stand in Your truth.

Remind me that I am defined by Your love, not by human opinion. Silence the enemy's lies that call me a failure. Guard my heart from bitterness toward those who criticize. Give me grace to respond with kindness when needed and wisdom to remain silent when words would only create more pain.

Strengthen me to keep walking in faith. Help me continue serving with confidence. Let my story—though marked with sorrow—point others to Your faithfulness. Cover me in Your peace and settle my heart in the approval of Christ alone.

In Jesus' name, Amen.

Affirmations

1. I live for God's approval, not man's.

2. I am not defined by my prodigal's choices.

3. Shame and condemnation have no authority over me.

4. I will not hide in fear; I will walk in freedom.

5. I do not need to explain my story to everyone; God knows my heart.

6. I will surround myself with safe and supportive people.

7. Criticism cannot shake me when I stand on God's truth.

8. My testimony will glorify God, even through pain.

9. Shame was broken at the cross of Christ.

10. I am covered, loved, and strengthened by the Lord.

Prayer Focus

- Pray for God to shield your heart from the opinions and judgments of others.

- Ask Him to replace shame with confidence in His love and approval.

- Pray for courage to stand firm in faith even when others misunderstand your situation.

- Thank God that your identity—and your prodigal's identity—is rooted in Christ, not in human judgment.

A Letter of Eternal Hope

My Dear [Child's/Grandchild's Name],

There have been moments when the opinions of others felt heavy—when whispers, looks, or comments about your choices cut deeply. Shame tried to convince me that your struggles were my failures. But hear me clearly: I will not let the voice of shame drown out the voice of truth.

You are not a label. You are not defined by mistakes, whether yours or mine. You are defined by God's love, His forgiveness, and His promise that your story is not over.

I will not bow to the judgment of others. I will bow only to the One who holds eternity in His hands. And I will keep lifting you to Him, believing that He is working even now to redeem every part of your life.

Always love you. Always here for you.
[Your Name]

Part III: Fighting the Battle

When love feels like a battlefield, prayer becomes your greatest weapon. These chapters will remind you that you are not powerless — you are armed with the promises of God. You'll learn how to pray with authority, stand firm against spiritual opposition, and release blessings over your family line. The war for your

prodigal's heart may rage fiercely, but victory belongs to the Lord.

Chapter 13:
Engaging in Spiritual Warfare

Behind every prodigal's journey is more than what you see with your eyes. There are spiritual battles being fought in unseen realms. Addiction, deception, rebellion, anger, and shame are not just bad habits or poor choices. They are strongholds the enemy uses to blind, bind, and hold your prodigal captive. Paul reminds us in Ephesians 6:12, "For we do not wrestle against flesh and blood, but against the rulers, against the authorities, against the cosmic powers over this present darkness, against the spiritual forces of evil in the heavenly places."

This means your prodigal is not your enemy. Even when their words wound you and their actions betray your love, the real enemy is Satan, who seeks to steal, kill, and destroy (John 10:10). Understanding this shifts your posture. You stop fighting against your prodigal and begin fighting for them in prayer.

Spiritual warfare is not about shouting at the darkness. It is about standing firm in the armor of God, wielding His Word as your sword, covering your family in prayer, and refusing to let the enemy claim victory. When the prodigal son was far away, his father stood watching, waiting, and praying. That waiting was not passive; it was warfare.

You may feel powerless, but in Christ you are armed. James 4:7 assures us, "Resist the devil, and he will flee from you." Every prayer you pray, every verse you declare, and every boundary you set in faith pushes back against the enemy's schemes. Your battle is not in vain.

Practical Guidance

1. **Recognize the true enemy**
   Your prodigal is not the enemy; Satan is. Separate their identity as God's beloved child from the strongholds that grip them.

2. **Put on the armor of God daily**
   Ephesians 6 calls you to wear the belt of truth, breastplate of righteousness, shield of faith, helmet of salvation, and sword of the Spirit. Pray each piece over yourself and your family.

3. **Use Scripture as a weapon**
   Declare God's promises aloud. Say, "No weapon formed against my child shall prosper" (Isaiah 54:17). The enemy cannot stand against the Word of God.

4. **Pray with authority in Jesus' name**
   Your prayers carry power because of Christ. In His name, resist fear, addiction, and deception, and invite peace, freedom, and truth into your prodigal's life.

5. **Fast and pray when led**
   Jesus said some strongholds break only through prayer and fasting (Mark 9:29). Seek God's direction and set aside time to fast for your prodigal.

6. **Protect your home spiritually**
   Pray over your house, anoint doorframes with oil, and dedicate every room to the Lord. Refuse to let the enemy's chaos rule your household.

7. **Pray in community**
   Join with others who know how to intercede. There is multiplied power when believers unite in prayer (Matthew 18:19–20).

8. **Stand firm, even when you do not see results**
   Warfare can feel long, but victory is certain in Christ. Do not quit praying. Perseverance is itself a weapon.

Prayer

Lord,

I thank You that the battle is Yours. I confess that I have often treated my prodigal as if they were the enemy, but today I recognize the truth: the real enemy is Satan, who seeks to destroy them. I choose to fight for my prodigal in prayer, not against them in anger.

I put on the full armor of God right now. I take up the shield of faith, the sword of the Spirit, and the helmet of salvation. I declare that no weapon formed against my prodigal will prosper. In the name of Jesus, I ask that every chain of addiction, deception, and rebellion be broken.

Cover my home with Your presence. Surround my family with Your angels. Fill me with perseverance when the battle feels long. Teach me to stand firm, not in my strength, but in the victory of the cross.

In Jesus' mighty name, Amen.

Affirmations

1. My prodigal is not my enemy; the devil is.

2. I am clothed in the full armor of God.

3. No weapon formed against my family will prosper.

4. The Word of God is my sword, and I will use it with power.

5. My prayers in Jesus' name carry authority.

6. Strongholds can be broken through prayer and fasting.

7. My home is covered and protected by the Lord.

8. I do not fight alone; heaven fights with me.

9. Perseverance in prayer is victory in action.

10. The battle belongs to the Lord, and victory is certain in Christ.

Prayer Focus

- Pray for discernment to recognize the enemy's lies and schemes against your prodigal.

- Ask God to arm you daily with His Word, His Spirit, and His strength.

- Declare the victory of Jesus Christ over your prodigal's life and over your family.

- Thank Him that the battle belongs to the Lord and that no weapon formed against your family will prevail.

A Letter of Eternal Hope

My Dear [Child's/Grandchild's Name],

I know that what you are facing is not just about choices or circumstances. It is a battle for your heart and soul. But I want you to know this: you are not alone in that fight. I am standing on my knees in prayer for you every single day.

The enemy may try to convince you that you are too far gone, too broken, or too trapped to be free. But I believe in a God who is stronger than every chain and greater than every darkness. Through Christ, the victory has already been won.

One day, I believe you will see how God has been fighting for you all along. Until then, I will keep declaring His promises over your life and reminding the enemy that he does not get the final word.

Always love you. Always here for you.
[Your Name]

Chapter 14:
Breaking Curses, Releasing Promises for Generations

Family patterns run deep. Addiction, anger, unbelief, poverty, fear, abuse, shame, and rebellion often echo through generations. What we saw in our parents, we sometimes see in ourselves and, painfully, in our children or grandchildren. It can feel like a curse you cannot shake—a cycle that keeps replaying no matter how much you pray or how deeply you hope things will change.

But the Word of God is clear: in Christ, the cycle can stop here. "Christ redeemed us from the curse of the law by becoming a curse for us" (Galatians 3:13). Through His blood, every generational chain—spoken or unspoken, known or hidden—can be broken.

You do not have to pass down what hurt you. You do not have to live under what enslaved your family. You are not doomed to repeat the past. Jesus paid the full price to free you and your descendants.

And God does more than stop curses. He releases promises. His blessings extend to a thousand generations of those who love Him (Deuteronomy 7:9). Every time you pray over your family and declare His Word over your home, you are helping rewrite a story the enemy tried to destroy.

Parent, grandparent—your prayers matter more than you realize. You are standing in the gap between what has been and what will be. By faith, you can close the door on curses and open the floodgates of blessing over your children and grandchildren.

Why Generational Curses Still Show Up

Curses are not mere superstition. They are patterns rooted in sin, trauma, and belief systems that contradict God's truth. They show up as repeated cycles: addiction that passes from father to son, fear that runs from mother to daughter, or shame that never seems to lift from a family's name.

Sometimes they begin with words spoken in anger or despair that take root in the heart. At other times they are inherited behaviors or spiritual strongholds left unchallenged. But here is the good news: you do not have to inherit what Jesus already conquered.

The cross breaks every claim of darkness. The blood of Jesus silences every accusation. What once was a curse can become a testimony of grace.

Practical Guidance

1. **Acknowledge what has been passed down**
   Do not deny the patterns. Name them and bring them to God. Pray, "Lord, I have seen anger, fear, addiction, and shame in our family, but I believe You can break them." What is confessed can be healed.

2. **Renounce every curse in Jesus' name**
   Speak with authority: "In the name of Jesus, I renounce and break every curse of fear, addiction, rebellion, and destruction. The blood of Jesus covers my family and ends this pattern today."

3. **Replace the curse with a blessing**
   God does not leave a void. After you break a curse, fill that

80

space with blessing. Speak life over your descendants: "My family will walk in peace, faith, integrity, and purpose."

4. **Guard what you speak**
   Life and death are in the power of the tongue (Proverbs 18:21). Do not repeat words of doom or despair. Replace "It has always been this way" with "God is rewriting our story."

5. **Pray Scripture over your lineage**
   Declare promises like Psalm 103:17, Deuteronomy 7:9, and Isaiah 54:17. Write them down. Say them aloud. Let your home be filled with God's Word instead of worry.

6. **Live the legacy you are praying for**
   Your family will follow what you live more than what you say. Let them see forgiveness, peace, and perseverance in you. Every act of faith plants seeds of blessing for those who come after you.

7. **Bless future generations by name**
   Bring your children, grandchildren, and even generations not yet born before God. Speak destiny over them. What you bless today becomes their inheritance tomorrow.

Prayer

Mighty God,
I stand in the gap for my family today. In the name of Jesus, I renounce and break every generational curse that has tried to rule over us: addiction, anger, unbelief, fear, shame, poverty, rebellion, abuse, sickness, and despair. These chains stop here. They will not pass on to my children or grandchildren.

The blood of Jesus covers our family line and silences every claim of the enemy. Where there has been bondage, release freedom. Where there has been anger, release peace. Where there has been unbelief, release faith. Where there has been despair, release joy.

Where there has been shame, release honor. Where there has been brokenness, release wholeness.

I declare that my children and grandchildren are not cursed; they are blessed. They are chosen, redeemed, and sealed by the Holy Spirit. Their story will not end in destruction but in victory through Christ.

Father, flood our family with generational blessings: faith that stands firm, love that never fails, joy that endures, wisdom that guides, protection that surrounds, and purpose that multiplies for generations not yet born.

In Jesus' mighty name, Amen.

Affirmations

1. The curse stops here; the blessing begins here.

2. My family is covered by the blood of Jesus.

3. Every generational stronghold is broken by His power.

4. My children and grandchildren are marked by God's promises, not past pain.

5. I am rewriting our family's story through prayer and faith.

6. What destroyed generations before will not destroy ours.

7. Our home will be known for peace, faith, and favor.

8. God's covenant blessings extend through my lineage.

9. Every dark root is replaced with light and truth.

10. Generational bondage has been exchanged for generational blessing.

Prayer Focus

- Pray and identify any repeating patterns in your family—spiritual, emotional, or relational—and surrender them to God.

- Declare freedom from those patterns in Jesus' name and replace each curse with a blessing.

- Pray daily over your children and grandchildren by name, speaking life, protection, and favor.

- Thank God for His covenant faithfulness that extends through your entire family line.

- Declare aloud:
  "What has plagued my family ends with me. What God begins with me will bless generations to come."

A Letter of Eternal Hope

My Dear [Child's/Grandchild's Name],

You are not bound by the past. Whatever brokenness has followed our family—addiction, fear, anger, or shame—has no ultimate power over you. Jesus broke those chains long before you ever took your first breath.

You were born for freedom, not bondage. You carry a new legacy, one rooted in grace and truth. Every prayer I pray over you is shaping a future filled with purpose, peace, and favor. You are covered by promises that were spoken before you even knew His name.

I believe God is rewriting our family story through you. You will be the generation that walks boldly in blessing, that turns darkness into light, and that proves God's faithfulness for those yet to come.

Always love you. Always here for you.
[Your Name]

Chapter 15:
Holding On to Hope

Hope can feel fragile when you are waiting for a prodigal. Days turn into weeks, weeks into years, and sometimes years into decades. Promises you believed would be fulfilled quickly seem delayed. Each relapse, harsh word, or silent holiday can feel like another crack in your faith. At times, hope feels like sand slipping through your fingers.

And yet hope is not a wish. Hope is not denial of pain or delay. Hope is an anchor. Hebrews 6:19 declares, "We have this as a sure and steadfast anchor of the soul, a hope that enters into the inner place behind the curtain." Hope is not based on what you see in your prodigal's life today; it is rooted in the unchanging character of God.

Abraham held on to hope for twenty-five years before Isaac was born, "hoping against hope" that God would do as He promised (Romans 4:18–21). Hannah prayed year after year for a child, enduring ridicule, yet she poured out her soul before the Lord until her miracle came (1 Samuel 1). Simeon waited his whole life to see the Messiah, and in his old age he finally held Him in his arms (Luke 2:25–32). Hope is not the absence of delay; it is the refusal to stop believing in God's timing.

When you hold on to hope, you are not pretending the pain is not real. You are declaring that the pain does not get the final word. You are planting your faith not in visible circumstances but in the invisible God who never fails. Even in seasons of waiting, hope

84

transforms you. It keeps you steady, strengthens your prayers, and reminds you that nothing surrendered to God is ever wasted.

Lamentations 3:21–23 reminds us, "But this I call to mind, and therefore I have hope: The steadfast love of the Lord never ceases; His mercies never come to an end; they are new every morning; great is Your faithfulness." Each new sunrise is a reminder that God has not abandoned you. His mercy is still flowing, His promises are still true, and His love is still active even when you cannot see it.

Practical Guidance

1. Anchor hope in God's character, not your prodigal's choices
   Circumstances change daily, but God's love and faithfulness never waver.

2. Feed hope with God's Word
   Write down promises of restoration and declare them aloud. Let Scripture be your daily anchor.

3. Celebrate small signs of grace
   A text, a softened tone, or a brief visit may not be the full breakthrough, but they are glimpses that God is still at work.

4. Guard against hopeless voices
   Limit time with those who only speak despair. Surround yourself with people who encourage faith.

5. Remember testimonies
   Read or listen to stories of prodigals who have returned. Testimonies remind you that what God did for others, He can do again.

6. Live today with purpose
   Do not put your entire life on hold while you wait. Serve,

love, and build your life in Christ, knowing He is faithful in every season.

7. Pray with expectancy
   Even if you see no evidence, pray believing that God can bring your prodigal home in His perfect time.

Prayer

Father,
I confess that sometimes hope feels hard to hold. My eyes see rebellion, my heart feels weary, and my prayers feel unanswered. But I choose today to anchor my hope not in circumstances but in You.

You are faithful. Your mercies are new every morning. Your love never fails. Even when I cannot see it, You are working. Even when I feel discouraged, You remain true.

Renew my hope today, Lord. Let me live expectantly, watching the horizon with faith. Guard me from despair and remind me of Your promises. Give me courage to wait, strength to endure, and joy in knowing You hold my prodigal's future in Your hands.

In Jesus' name, Amen.

Affirmations

1. My hope is anchored in God's faithfulness, not my prodigal's choices.

2. God's mercies are new every morning.

3. I will not let despair steal my vision of God's power.

4. Even small signs remind me that God is at work.

5. I will surround myself with voices that speak faith and encouragement.

6. My waiting is not wasted; God is working in unseen ways.

7. Testimonies remind me that God still restores.

8. I can live today with joy and purpose while I wait.

9. Prayer keeps my hope alive and connected to God's promises.

10. Hope will not disappoint me, because God's love never fails (Romans 5:5).

Prayer Focus

- Pray for endurance when hope feels small or far away.

- Ask God to renew your vision daily, reminding you of His promises for your prodigal.

- Declare by faith that God is still working, even in silence and waiting.

- Thank Him that hope is not based on what you see but on who He is.

A Letter of Eternal Hope

My Dear [Child's/Grandchild's Name],

There are days when holding on feels hard. I have cried, I have prayed, and I have waited longer than I ever imagined. But no matter how long it takes, I will not let go of hope.

I believe God is still writing your story. Even when I do not see change, I know He is moving behind the scenes. Even when my heart feels weary, I know His Word is true. And even when it looks impossible, I know nothing is too hard for Him.

Hope is not just wishful thinking; it is the anchor of my soul. And I am holding on with both hands for you, believing that one day we will rejoice together in all that God has done.

Always love you. Always here for you.
[Your Name]

Chapter 16:
The Power of Community

Loving a prodigal can feel incredibly lonely. You may sit in church surrounded by smiling families and wonder if anyone else understands the ache in your heart. You may dread questions from friends or avoid gatherings altogether because the pain feels too heavy to explain. The enemy whispers that you are alone in your struggle, but that is a lie.

From the very beginning, God designed us for community. "It is not good that the man should be alone" (Genesis 2:18). The church was born as a family of believers bearing one another's burdens. Galatians 6:2 commands us, "Bear one another's burdens, and so fulfill the law of Christ." Even Moses needed Aaron and Hur to hold up his arms in battle when he grew weary (Exodus 17:12). We are not called to carry our pain in isolation; we are called to lean on one another.

Community provides what isolation cannot: prayer when your words run out, encouragement when despair closes in, and accountability when bitterness threatens to take root. In safe community, you find people who do not minimize your pain, who listen without judgment, and who remind you that God is still faithful.

Your prodigal's journey may not change overnight, but walking with others who believe with you makes the waiting lighter. Ecclesiastes 4:12 says, "A threefold cord is not quickly broken." You,

89

your brothers and sisters in Christ, and the Spirit of God together form a cord of strength that can withstand storms.

Practical Guidance

1. **Seek out safe people**
   Find a prayer partner, mentor, or small group where you can be honest. Look for those who listen with compassion and carry hope.

2. **Join supportive groups**
   Consider joining a prodigal prayer group, Christian support group, or intercessory team where your burden is shared.

3. **Let others in**
   Share your story selectively with trusted people. Vulnerability invites intercession.

4. **Serve while you wait**
   Pouring into others can bring healing. Serving widows, youth, or the hurting reminds you that your pain has purpose and that you are not forgotten.

5. **Ask for prayer boldly**
   Do not hesitate to say, "Please pray for my prodigal." Your request may inspire others to believe for their own families.

6. **Reject isolation**
   The enemy thrives when you withdraw. Even if you feel awkward or tired, choose connection over loneliness.

7. **Celebrate together**
   When God moves—whether in your prodigal's life or someone else's—celebrate with your community. Their testimonies strengthen your hope.

Prayer

Father,

Thank You for creating me to live in fellowship and not in isolation. Forgive me for the times I have pulled away in shame or despair. Surround me with people who will encourage me, pray for me, and stand with me as I wait for my prodigal.

Help me to open my heart and share my burden wisely. Let me also be a source of encouragement to others, so that we may carry one another's burdens and point each other back to You. Knit me into a cord of strength with other believers, and let us stand together in hope.

In Jesus' name, Amen.

Affirmations

1. I am not alone; God has given me safe people to walk with.
2. Sharing my burden invites strength and intercession.
3. Isolation is the enemy's tool; connection is God's gift.
4. Community reminds me that hope is still alive.
5. I will both receive encouragement and give it to others.
6. My story can inspire someone else not to give up.
7. Together we are stronger, like a threefold cord.
8. I choose to walk in fellowship instead of loneliness.
9. Prayer partners multiply my strength in the battle.
10. God is glorified when His people carry one another's burdens.

Prayer Focus

- Pray for God to surround you with a strong, faith-filled community that will stand with you in prayer.

- Ask Him to protect you from isolation and remind you that you do not have to walk this journey alone.

- Pray for your prodigal to encounter godly influences—friends, mentors, pastors—who will point them back to Christ.

- Thank God for the body of Christ, the family of faith, who can help carry the burden when it feels too heavy.

A Letter of Eternal Hope

My Dear [Child's/Grandchild's Name],

You may not realize it, but there are many people besides me who are praying for you, cheering for you, and waiting to see God's story unfold in your life. We were never meant to walk this road alone, and I am so thankful for the community of faith that stands with me as I pray for you.

Someday, I believe you will look around and see how many people have loved you, prayed for you, and welcomed you with open arms. You are not forgotten, and you are not alone. God has surrounded you with more love than you know.

Until the day your eyes are opened to that truth, I will continue to pray that you feel the pull of His people and the embrace of His love drawing you back home.

Always love you. Always here for you.
[Your Name]

Chapter 17:
The God Who Redeems

Redemption is at the heart of God's character. What the enemy means for harm, God turns into good (Genesis 50:20). What seems wasted, God restores. What looks beyond repair, God rebuilds.

Loving a prodigal often leaves you feeling as if years have been lost: missed birthdays, broken relationships, fractured holidays, and memories that ache instead of bring joy. You may look back and wonder if anything good can come from the heartbreak. But God's Word assures you that nothing is wasted in His hands.

Think of Joseph, sold by his brothers, falsely accused, and forgotten in prison. Years of his life were taken from him, yet at the end he could say to those who wronged him, "You meant evil against me, but God meant it for good, to bring it about that many people should be kept alive" (Genesis 50:20). Joseph's suffering was not wasted; it became the very stage for God's redemption.

Think of Naomi, who returned to Bethlehem bitter and empty after losing her husband and sons. Yet through Ruth, the outsider who chose faith, God restored her family line and made Naomi part of the story of King David and ultimately Jesus Himself (Ruth 4:14–17).

God does not simply return what was lost. He brings back more than before. Joel 2:25 declares, "I will restore to you the years that the swarming locust has eaten." His redemption does not erase

93

the pain, but it transforms it into testimony, beauty, and eternal fruit.

No matter how far your prodigal has gone, no matter how much damage has been done, no matter how many years feel wasted, you serve a God who redeems.

Practical Guidance

1. **Remember God's track record**
   Revisit stories of redemption in Scripture—Joseph, Naomi, Paul, the prodigal son—and remind yourself: the God who redeemed them can redeem you and your family.

2. **Look for glimpses of restoration**
   Redemption often begins in small ways: a softened heart, a moment of honesty, or even a fresh sense of God's peace in your own spirit.

3. **Surrender the "wasted" years**
   Instead of mourning only what is lost, release those years into God's hands. Ask Him to bring fruit you cannot yet see.

4. **Allow God to redeem your pain for others**
   Your testimony may become the lifeline someone else needs. Share your story when God prompts you.

5. **Pray boldly for full restoration**
   Do not be afraid to ask God to redeem relationships, heal wounds, and rewrite broken storylines in your family.

6. **Hold loosely to your timetable**
   God's redemption may not come quickly, but it always comes fully. Trust His timing.

7. **Keep hope alive through worship**
   Singing and declaring God's goodness, even in pain, positions your heart to see His redemption more clearly.

Prayer

Father,
Thank You that You are the God who redeems. When I see brokenness, You see restoration. When I see wasted years, You see seeds of eternal fruit. When I feel loss, You promise to bring beauty from ashes.

I surrender my prodigal, my family, and my own heart into Your hands. Redeem the years that feel wasted. Restore relationships that feel broken. Heal wounds that seem too deep to mend. Use even my pain as part of Your testimony of grace.

Help me to trust that You are always working for good, even when I cannot see it. Let my life declare that nothing is too far gone, nothing is too broken, and no story is beyond Your redemption.

In Jesus' name, Amen.

Affirmations

1. God redeems what feels wasted.

2. What the enemy meant for harm, God will use for good.

3. My prodigal is not beyond God's power to restore.

4. The years that feel lost will be restored in God's timing.

5. God is writing beauty out of ashes in my family's story.

6. My pain will become part of someone else's healing.

7. Redemption is God's specialty; He never leaves a story unfinished.

8. I will trust His timing, not my own.

9. Restoration is possible because God is faithful.

10. My legacy will be marked by redemption, not despair.

Prayer Focus

- Pray for your prodigal to encounter God's redeeming love in a personal and undeniable way.

- Ask the Lord to transform what the enemy meant for harm into a testimony of His grace.

- Pray for your own heart to rest in the truth that God specializes in restoration, no matter how broken the situation.

- Thank Him that redemption is His nature and that your prodigal's story is not beyond His reach.

A Letter of Eternal Hope

My Dear [Child's/Grandchild's Name],

When I look at your journey, I see mistakes and scars, yes, but more than that, I see the fingerprints of a God who redeems. He is not finished with you. Every wrong turn can be rewritten. Every broken piece can be restored. Every failure can become part of a testimony of grace.

You are not beyond redemption. No one is. The cross proves that love goes further than sin and mercy reaches deeper than shame. I believe one day you will stand and tell the story of how God turned your ashes into beauty and your pain into purpose.

Until that day, I will keep holding on to the Redeemer who loves us both more than we can imagine.

Always love you. Always here for you.
[Your Name]

Part IV: Living Beyond the Waiting

One day, the waiting will end. Even while you wait, there is life to be lived, joy to be found, and peace to be restored. These final chapters will help you live with purpose again, care for your own soul, and celebrate the quiet victories along the way. The story is not over. God is still writing, redeeming, and restoring. Hope still lives, and His promises still stand.

Chapter 18:
Leaving a Legacy of Faith

When you love a prodigal, it is easy to feel as if your influence has faded into silence. You have prayed, spoken truth, and tried to lead by example, but the results seem invisible. You may wonder, "Did any of it matter? Did they hear me? Did they see God in me?"

Heaven has heard every prayer. Not one seed of faith you have planted has been wasted. God has woven your love, prayers, and faithfulness into a story that will outlive you. The legacy you leave is not determined by what your prodigal does today; it is shaped by what you keep believing God will do tomorrow.

You are not losing influence; you are building a foundation. Every Scripture spoken, every act of kindness, every whispered prayer becomes a brick in a legacy of faith that God Himself is strengthening. He multiplies the unseen moments: the prayers in the night, the tears in the dark, the steadfast love that keeps showing up.

Psalm 126:5–6 promises, "Those who sow in tears shall reap with shouts of joy! He who goes out weeping, bearing the seed for sowing, shall come home with shouts of joy, bringing his sheaves with him." Your tears are not a sign of weakness; they are holy water on the soil of your family's future.

The Bible is filled with stories of faith passed through generations:

98

- Lois and Eunice, whose steady example helped raise Timothy into a pillar of the early church (2 Timothy 1:5).

- Abraham, whose covenant promise stretched far beyond his lifetime (Genesis 17:7).

- David, whose legacy of worship and repentance shaped a royal line that led to Jesus Himself (2 Samuel 7:16).

Their faith outlived them, and so will yours. Your legacy is not erased by your prodigal's rebellion; it is refined by it. God is using even the hard chapters to write a testimony of His redemption through your family line.

Legacy is not about perfection; it is about perseverance. It is about choosing faith over fear, hope over despair, and love over bitterness. It is about leaving behind a trail of light and truth that those who come after you can follow all the way home to Jesus.

Scriptures to Declare

- "Those who sow in tears shall reap with shouts of joy." — Psalm 126:5

- "I am reminded of your sincere faith, a faith that dwelt first in your grandmother Lois and your mother Eunice." — 2 Timothy 1:5

- "I will establish my covenant between me and you and your offspring after you." — Genesis 17:7

- "The righteous who walks in his integrity—blessed are his children after him." — Proverbs 20:7

Prayer

Father,
Thank You for the faith You have placed in me. Even when my heart aches for my prodigal, I trust that my prayers, love, and obedience are not wasted.

Let my life be a seed that grows into a harvest of faith in my children and grandchildren. Restore what is broken in our family line and raise up future generations who walk in Your truth.

Teach me to model steady faith in both joy and sorrow. Let my words bless, my actions inspire, and my example shine as a light. When I leave this world, may my legacy still whisper to those I love: "Keep trusting God. He is faithful."

In Jesus' name, Amen.

Practical Guidance

1. **Pray generational prayers**
   Ask God not only to save your prodigal but to awaken faith in your children, grandchildren, and great-grandchildren. Pray that your family line will be marked by revival.

2. **Be faithful in the small things**
   Simple acts—reading Scripture, blessing meals, showing kindness—create rhythms of faith that are remembered long after words fade.

3. **Create written records of faith**
   Keep prayer journals, write legacy letters, or record testimonies. Even if ignored now, these words may one day draw your prodigal home.

4. **Speak blessing over your family**
   Declare God's promises aloud. "Death and life are in the power of the tongue" (Proverbs 18:21). Use your words to plant life.

5. **Live with hope, not bitterness**
   Choose forgiveness and joy. Bitterness poisons legacy, but hope leaves a fragrance that lingers.

6. **Pass down tangible faith markers**
   Give family Bibles with notes, Scripture plaques, or heirlooms tied to God's faithfulness. Physical reminders keep spiritual truths alive.

7. **Tell the stories**
   Share testimonies of how God answered prayers in the past. Your stories become the treasure map of your family's faith.

8. **Model perseverance**
   Keep praying, even when results seem distant. Perseverance preaches louder than perfection.

Prayer Focus

- Pray that your life will become testimony future generations remember.

- Ask God to remove bitterness and replace it with joy as you sow in faith.

- Thank Him that His covenant love extends to your children's children.

- Declare that your family line will be known for faith, restoration, and blessing.

Affirmations

1. My faith is shaping generations I may never meet.

2. My prayers are eternal seeds that will bear fruit.

3. God redeems family lines, and mine will be restored.

4. I choose perseverance over despair.

5. I will speak blessing, not curses, over my family.

6. My faith will leave a trail for my prodigal to follow home.

7. Bitterness will not mark my legacy; hope will.

8. God's promises extend beyond my lifetime.

9. Even in tears, I am sowing for a future harvest.

10. My legacy will glorify God for generations to come.

A Letter of Eternal Hope

My Dear [Child's/Grandchild's Name],

There is so much I want for you—not just success or happiness, but a faith that lasts. Even when you have wandered, my love and prayers have followed you. I have asked God to make our family line one that walks in His truth and carries His grace.

You may not see it now, but you are part of something bigger than this moment. The prayers I have prayed and the seeds of faith I have sown are not lost. They are growing quietly, waiting for the right season to bloom in your life.

I believe one day you will walk in the blessings that have been prayed over you. When you do, I hope you will pass them on—to your children, and to theirs.

Always love you. Always here for you.
[Your Name]

Chapter 19:
A Future and a Hope

Loving a prodigal can sometimes feel like standing in the ruins of a dream. You look at broken trust, years of rebellion, unanswered prayers, and you wonder: *Is there really a future left for us?* Yet God's Word thunders across the ages:

"For I know the plans I have for you, declares the Lord, plans for welfare and not for evil, to give you a future and a hope" (Jeremiah 29:11).

This promise was not given to people who had everything together. It was given to God's people in exile—far from home, grieving loss, and uncertain of tomorrow. And still, God said: "I know the plans I have for you." His plans did not end in exile. They did not end in despair. They were plans to restore, rebuild, and redeem.

Maybe you feel like you are living in your own exile. Holidays filled with absence. Phone calls that never come. Words that cut deep. Years that feel wasted. But exile is not the end of your story. The God who promised Israel a future is the same God who promises you one.

God specializes in turning ashes into beauty (Isaiah 61:3), dry bones into living armies (Ezekiel 37:1–10), and graves into gardens (John 11). He takes what looks dead and breathes resurrection life into it.

Think of Joseph, who endured betrayal, slavery, and prison, yet in the end became the rescuer of nations. Think of Job, who lost

103

everything, and yet God restored him with double blessing. Think of Peter, who denied Christ three times, but was restored to become a pillar of the early church.

If God could write a future for Joseph, Job, and Peter, He can write one for your prodigal—and for you.

Isaiah 43:19 declares:

"Behold, I am doing a new thing; now it springs forth, do you not perceive it? I will make a way in the wilderness and rivers in the desert."

Where you see only wasteland, God sees new growth. Where you see only desert, God promises streams of life.

The future God has planned is not limited by your prodigal's rebellion, your mistakes as a parent, or the opinions of others. His future is anchored in His mercy, His redemption, and His power to restore what has been lost.

Holding on to hope for the future does not mean denying present pain. It means believing that pain does not get the final word. Your prodigal's story is still unfolding, and God is still writing chapters that you cannot yet see.

Practical Guidance

1. **Declare God's promises daily**
   Speak Jeremiah 29:11, Isaiah 43:19, and Romans 8:28 over your prodigal's life, even when circumstances look unchanged.

2. **Prophesy over the future**
   Speak life into your prodigal's destiny: "You will rise. You will return. You will know the Lord." Your words carry power (Proverbs 18:21).

3. **Envision restoration**
   Picture your prodigal walking with God. Imagine family

104

gatherings healed by grace. Let hope shape your vision of the future.

4. **Plant seeds for tomorrow**
   Keep praying, keep serving, and keep sowing kindness. What you plant now will grow into a harvest later.

5. **Release the past fully**
   You cannot grasp the new thing while clinging to regrets. Give God the ashes and let Him give you beauty in return.

6. **Worship while you wait**
   Worship shifts despair into expectation. Even in exile, the Israelites sang songs of faith. Sing your way into hope.

7. **Live in anticipation, not fear**
   Begin preparing your heart for restoration as if it is certain—because in Christ, it is.

8. **Keep eternity in view**
   Even if the full restoration doesn't come in your lifetime, eternity guarantees the story ends in victory.

Prayer

Father,
I lift my eyes from the ruins and fix them on Your promises. I declare that exile is not the end. Brokenness is not final. Despair does not have the last word.

You are the God who makes rivers in the desert and pathways in the wilderness. Where I see nothing but wasteland, You see new growth. Where I see death, You see resurrection. Where I see despair, You are planting hope.

Lord, I speak life over my prodigal: they will not remain in rebellion forever. I declare that Your Spirit is pursuing them, that Your mercy is surrounding them, and that Your plans for them are good.

Redeem the years that feel wasted. Restore the joy that has been stolen. Renew my hope when I am weary. And let my family's story declare to the world: "The Lord is faithful."

I will live with anticipation, not despair. I will sow in faith, even when I do not see the harvest. And I will cling to Your Word, because You are not a man that You should lie. Your promises are Yes and Amen.

In Jesus' mighty name, Amen.

Affirmations

1. God's plans for my family are good, not evil.

2. Exile is not the end; restoration is coming.

3. God is writing a future I cannot yet see.

4. My prodigal's story is not over.

5. Hope is my inheritance in Christ.

6. God makes a way in the wilderness and rivers in the desert.

7. The years that feel wasted will be redeemed.

8. I refuse despair; I choose expectation.

9. I will see the goodness of the Lord in the land of the living (Psalm 27:13).

10. My hope is alive because my Redeemer lives.

11. Every seed I plant today will bear fruit tomorrow.

12. I live with eyes on eternity, where every story ends in victory.

Prayer Focus

- Pray that your life will reflect a legacy of faith, hope, and love for your prodigal and future generations.

- Ask God to help you sow seeds of truth and blessing into your family, even if you don't see the harvest right away.

- Pray for the courage to model forgiveness, perseverance, and trust in God's promises.

- Thank Him that your faith is not wasted—that it will outlive you and bless generations to come.

A Letter of Eternal Hope

My Dear [Child's/Grandchild's Name],

More than anything, I want to leave you a legacy—not of wealth or possessions, but of faith. When my time on earth is over, I pray you will remember that I believed for you even in the darkest moments, that I trusted God when circumstances gave me every reason not to, and that I prayed for you without ceasing.

You are part of a bigger story, one that began long before you and will continue long after us. My hope is that my prayers, my faith, and my love will be like stones laid on a path that lead you closer to Jesus.

One day, I believe you will see how much of your life has been shaped by the prayers spoken over you and the promises of God passed down to you. That will be the true inheritance I leave you: the knowledge that God is faithful, and your story is still being written by His hand.

Always love you. Always here for you.
[Your Name]

Chapter 20:
When the Prodigal
Doesn't Return Home

There are no words that fully capture the sorrow of realizing your prodigal may not return in this life. It is a grief unlike any other—the ache of unanswered prayers, the longing for reconciliation that never came, the empty seat at the table that still feels occupied by hope. It's the silent wondering: *Did I do enough? Could I have said more? Why didn't they come home?*

For some, this moment comes after years of waiting. The phone call doesn't come. The knock on the door never happens. And then suddenly, there's news—an accident, an overdose, a heart attack, a tragedy that stops everything. In the silence that follows, you feel the weight of a thousand unspoken words.

For others, the loss is quieter. The prodigal is still alive, but emotionally gone—estranged, distant, unreachable. They have built walls so high that reconciliation feels impossible. They have moved on, living a life apart from God and from you. You still see glimpses of them—perhaps through social media or a passing comment from someone who has crossed their path—but the bond that once felt unbreakable now feels like a memory. You grieve a person who still walks the earth but no longer shares your heart.

Both forms of loss—the physical and the emotional—cut deeply. You replay old memories, analyze every word ever spoken,

108

and question your prayers. Grief collides with guilt, and faith wrestles with finality. Yet even here, even in this valley of sorrow, God's promises remain true.

David knew this kind of heartbreak. He wept and fasted for his child, begging God for mercy, but when the child died, he rose and said, "I shall go to him, but he will not return to me" (2 Samuel 12:23). There are moments when the answer we long for does not come on this side of eternity. And still, faith remains. Hebrews 11 reminds us that many of the heroes of faith "died in faith, not having received the things promised, but having seen them and greeted them from afar." Faith is not proven by seeing the outcome—it is proven by continuing to trust the One who holds it.

Some prodigals leave this world suddenly—through tragedy, addiction, or illness. Others drift slowly, choosing a life apart from God, cutting off the people who love them most. Some pass away without you ever knowing if they turned back to the Lord. These are the questions that haunt the quiet hours of the night. But even in what feels unfinished, God's mercy is not. His love reaches further than our sight. The thief on the cross is proof that grace can reach the soul in its final breath. One whispered prayer, "Jesus, remember me," was enough to secure eternity. You may never know what happened in those last moments of your prodigal's life—but God does.

And for those whose prodigals are still alive but far away, God's reach is not shortened by silence or distance. You may not see them change, but your prayers still carry power. The Holy Spirit continues to move in places your voice cannot go. Heaven's story doesn't end where your communication stops.

So what do you do when the waiting ends in loss, or when reconciliation never comes?

You start by giving yourself permission to grieve. God can handle your tears, your anger, and your questions. He met Mary and

Martha in their grief and wept with them. Grieving is not a sign of weak faith—it is evidence of love.

Don't let guilt rewrite the story. You loved your prodigal. You prayed faithfully. You fought with everything you had. Only God can save a soul, and you were never meant to carry what belongs to Him.

Even when you didn't see repentance, God may have met your prodigal in their final thought, their quietest moment, or their last heartbeat. His mercy stretches beyond our comprehension. And if your prodigal has simply drifted away, still choosing rebellion or distance, know this: the story isn't over. God's timing doesn't end with ours. He is still working in unseen ways, and eternity is long enough for redemption to reach every lost heart.

Keep living with purpose. Don't let grief steal your calling. Your story continues, even when theirs seems paused. Love others in their pain. Serve with compassion. Let your testimony become light for those walking through darkness. Remember your prodigal with tenderness, but don't let sorrow define you. Their memory can live as a seed of hope in your ministry to others who are still waiting.

And keep your eyes on heaven. One day you may both be in heaven worshiping God. Revelation 21:4 promises, "He will wipe away every tear from their eyes, and death shall be no more." One day, the ache will be gone, the distance erased, and the story complete. Until then, walk with peace. Trust that no life, no prayer, and no love offered in Christ is ever wasted.

God is still the Author of resurrection stories. The tomb is empty, and that truth means every "ending" you face is temporary. The same power that raised Jesus from the dead is still at work in your story—and in your prodigal's.

So release the guilt. Let go of the "what ifs." Breathe in the mercy that still holds both of you. You are not alone. God is with you in the silence, the sorrow, and the surrender. And in His hands, no story is ever truly lost.

Practical Guidance

1. **Allow yourself to grieve deeply**
   Do not minimize your sorrow. Pour it out before God in honesty—lament is worship too.

2. **Release the burden of responsibility**
   You are not your prodigal's Savior. Their salvation is between them and Christ. You were faithful; now rest in God's justice and mercy.

3. **Trust in last-moment mercy**
   Remember the thief on the cross—redemption is possible even at the final breath.

4. **Fix your eyes on eternity**
   Let heaven's reality comfort you. This life is not the whole story.

5. **Leave a legacy in their honor**
   Write your prayers, share your testimony, or serve others in your prodigal's memory. Let your pain become purpose.

6. **Let God redeem even this**
   He promises to bring beauty from ashes. Even the ashes of grief can become a testimony of His comfort.

7. **Keep living with open hands**
   Don't let sorrow consume your whole life. Let hope continue shaping the future God still has for you.

Prayer

Father,
This is the hardest prayer I have ever prayed. My heart feels broken beyond repair as I face the reality that my prodigal did not return as I had hoped. I confess my questions, my grief, and the ache of all that feels unfinished.

Yet I trust You. You are merciful and just. You are the God who hears whispers in the dark and saves to the uttermost. Where I cannot go, You can. Where I cannot see, You see. Where my story feels cut short, Yours continues forever.

I release my prodigal into Your hands fully. Redeem what I cannot redeem. Heal what I cannot heal. Write chapters in eternity that my eyes could not see in this life. And Lord, redeem my pain—let my tears become seeds of hope for others.

I look to the day when You will wipe every tear from my eyes and sorrow will be no more. Until then, hold me close and remind me that You are still faithful.

In Jesus' name, Amen.

Affirmations

1. My prayers are not wasted—they live before God like incense.

2. I release the burden of salvation into God's hands.

3. Eternity is long, and God's story is not finished.

4. Redemption is possible even in a final breath.

5. My legacy of faith continues beyond this life.

6. I grieve honestly, but not without eternal hope.

7. My sorrow will become a testimony of God's comfort.

8. Heaven is my ultimate reunion, where every tear will be wiped away.

9. God's faithfulness is not limited to what I can see.

10. I will live with hope, even in grief, because God is still writing the story.

Prayer Focus

- Pray for God's peace to cover the grief of unanswered prayers in this lifetime.

- Ask Him to remind you that His mercy reaches further than your eyes could see—even into the final moments of life.

- Pray against the lies of regret and condemnation that whisper, "You didn't do enough."

- Thank Him for eternity, where every tear will be wiped away and every story will be fully redeemed.

A Letter of Eternal Hope

My Dear [Child's/Grandchild's Name],

I prayed for you every day, longing to see the moment when you would come back to God while I was still here to witness it. That moment never came in my lifetime, and my heart grieves the empty seat, the missed conversations, and the hug I didn't get to give.

But my hope does not die with time. I believe God's mercy reached for you in ways I could not see. Even in your final hours, He was near. I cling to the truth that He is faithful, that He hears even the faintest prayer, and that eternity holds what this life could not give us.

I trust that your story was never out of His hands. And I believe the reunion I longed for may not happen here, but it will happen in heaven—where there is no more sorrow, no more pain, and no more tears.

Always love you. Always here for you.
[Your Name]

Chapter 21:
Caring for Yourself
in the Journey

When you love a prodigal, the weight of worry, prayer, and heartbreak can slowly consume you until there is almost nothing left. Sleepless nights, anxious thoughts, and constant tension wear you down little by little. Before long, exhaustion feels normal and despair whispers that you are too weak to go on.

But God never asked you to carry this burden alone or to destroy yourself in the process. Jesus said, "Come to me, all who labor and are heavy laden, and I will give you rest" (Matthew 11:28). Rest is not selfish. Renewal is not indulgent. Caring for yourself is an act of obedience, because it honors the truth that your life and body belong to God.

Even Elijah, after his great victory on Mount Carmel, collapsed in despair and prayed to die. What did God do? He did not rebuke Elijah for weakness. He sent an angel with food, water, and the command to rest (1 Kings 19:5–8). Only after Elijah was restored did God send him back to continue the mission.

If a prophet needed rest and care, so do you. Self-care in this journey is not abandoning your prodigal; it is stewarding your life so you can endure, pray, and love with strength. A weary soul cannot fight well. A broken body cannot stand in the gap. A discouraged heart struggles to intercede with faith.

Caring for yourself is not stepping away from the battle. It is sharpening your sword for the long fight.

Scriptures to Declare

- "Come to me, all who labor and are heavy laden, and I will give you rest." — Matthew 11:28

- "But they who wait for the Lord shall renew their strength; they shall mount up with wings like eagles; they shall run and not be weary; they shall walk and not faint." — Isaiah 40:31

- "He makes me lie down in green pastures. He leads me beside still waters. He restores my soul." — Psalm 23:2–3

- "In returning and rest you shall be saved; in quietness and in trust shall be your strength." — Isaiah 30:15

Prayer

Father,
I confess that I have tried to carry this weight in my own strength, and I am weary. My body feels drained, my mind clouded, and my spirit heavy. Today I come to You just as Jesus invited me: tired, burdened, and in need of rest.

Teach me to rest without guilt. Remind me that I am also Your child—loved, seen, and cared for. Refresh my body with health, my mind with peace, and my spirit with joy. Help me walk in rhythms of grace instead of cycles of exhaustion.

Let my self-care be an act of faith, not failure. As I care for myself, strengthen me to pray more boldly, love more deeply, and endure more faithfully. Renew my strength like the eagle's so I may run and not grow weary, walk and not faint.

In Jesus' name,
Amen.

Practical Guidance

1. **Prioritize rest without guilt**
   Sleep is sacred. Protect your rest and embrace Sabbath rhythms. Even Jesus withdrew to quiet places (Luke 5:16).

2. **Nourish your body wisely**
   Eat balanced meals. Hydrate. Move gently—walk, stretch, breathe deeply. Your body is the temple of the Holy Spirit.

3. **Make exercise a prayer**
   Walk and talk with God. Let movement become worship, releasing stress and inviting His peace into your body.

4. **Guard your mental space**
   Limit endless scrolling, comparison, and negative media. Fill your mind with Scripture, worship, and gratitude (Philippians 4:8).

5. **Tend to emotional health**
   Talk with a trusted friend, pastor, or counselor. Journal honestly. Allow yourself to cry. Tears release pain that words cannot.

6. **Practice Sabbath rhythms**
   Schedule moments for joy: reading, gardening, worship, creativity, or laughter. Renewal restores perspective and refuels perseverance.

7. **Release false guilt**
   Resting does not mean neglecting your prodigal. It means trusting that God works even when you are still.

8. **Ask God to refresh your spirit daily**
   Begin each morning with a simple prayer: "Lord, fill me again with Your strength and peace for today."

Prayer Focus

- Pray that God renews your strength daily and helps you create healthy rhythms of rest.

- Ask Him to replace anxiety with peace and guilt with grace.

- Pray for the courage to set healthy boundaries without fear.

- Thank God that while you rest, He is still working on behalf of your prodigal.

Affirmations

1. Rest is holy, and I will honor it without guilt.

2. My body is God's temple, and I will care for it.

3. Exercise refreshes my body and clears my spirit.

4. My emotions are safe in God's hands.

5. My mind will be filled with truth, not despair.

6. Self-care equips me to endure with faith.

7. I am worthy of rest because I am God's beloved child.

8. My strength will be renewed daily by the Lord.

9. I will celebrate small joys as gifts of grace.

10. My hope is sustained when I refresh my soul.

A Letter of Eternal Hope

My Dear [Child's/Grandchild's Name],

There are days when loving you has left me weary. I have carried heavy burdens and prayed prayers that felt like whispers in the dark. But even in the weariness, I have learned something beautiful: God sustains me.

I have discovered that caring for myself does not mean I have stopped caring for you. It means I have learned to trust God to do what I cannot. It means I have learned that love is stronger when it rests in His strength instead of mine.

As I find rest in Him, I find hope again—for me and for you. And I pray that one day you too will learn the peace that comes from letting God carry what was never yours to hold alone.

Always love you. Always here for you.
[Your Name]

Chapter 22:
What We Carry Forward

The journey of loving a prodigal is not easy. It is filled with heartbreak, waiting, and tears. It can feel lonely and heavy, yet it is also a path where God meets you with His presence, His promises, and His power.

You have walked through grief and brokenness, learned how to pray with power, faced shame and judgment, established boundaries, and lifted your eyes to the God who redeems. You have discovered that hope is an anchor, that community is essential, and that legacy is bigger than one lifetime. You have faced the reality that some prodigals may not return in this life, yet you cling to the truth that eternity is not bound by what you see.

Through it all, one truth remains: God is faithful. He is faithful to hear every prayer, collect every tear, redeem every loss, and write every story. Your role has never been to fix your prodigal. It has always been to trust, pray, and love as God carries them.

As you step forward from these pages, remember this: you are not alone. You are part of a great cloud of witnesses—parents and grandparents across generations—who have prayed, believed, and stood for their children. You are part of God's unfolding story, and your faith is leaving a mark on generations yet to come.

Your prodigal's story is not over. Neither is yours. God is still writing. And in His hands, the ending will always be good.

Practical Guidance

1. **Revisit these pages often**
   Let the prayers, Scriptures, and affirmations continue to strengthen you.

2. **Live day by day in grace**
   Do not carry tomorrow's burden today. Trust God for each new sunrise.

3. **Keep hope alive**
   Even when you do not see results, know that God is working in unseen ways.

4. **Stay in community**
   Lean on those who believe with you, and be that encourager for someone else.

5. **Leave a trail of faith**
   Write down prayers, speak blessings, and let your faith ripple into generations.

Prayer

Father,
Thank You for walking with me through this journey. Thank You that I am not alone, that my prayers matter, and that You are faithful. I place my prodigal in Your hands again today, trusting You to finish what You have begun.

Bless every parent and grandparent who walks this road. Strengthen them when they are weak, comfort them when they weep, and renew their hope each morning. Let their lives leave a legacy of faith that testifies to Your power and love.

Lord, we declare together: our prodigals are not too far, our prayers are not too small, and Your mercy is not finished. Their story is not over, because You are still writing.

In Jesus' mighty name, Amen.

Affirmations

1. I am not alone—God walks this journey with me.
2. My prayers are powerful and eternal.
3. Hope is my anchor, and I will not let it go.
4. My prodigal is not beyond God's reach.
5. Every tear I have sown will reap joy in God's time.
6. My legacy of faith will outlive me.
7. Even in grief, I cling to eternal hope.
8. God is faithful yesterday, today, and forever.
9. The story is not over—God is still writing.
10. I will live with expectation, not despair.

Prayer Focus

- Pray for God's comfort to surround you when grief feels heavier than hope.
- Ask Him to anchor your faith in eternity, trusting that He writes chapters beyond this lifetime.
- Pray against despair, declaring that your prayers and love were never wasted.
- Thank Him that His mercy reaches further than you ever could, even into the final moments of life.

A Letter of Eternal Hope

My Dear [Child's/Grandchild's Name],

If I could have chosen the story, you would have come home to God while I was still here to see it. I longed for the day when I could hold you close, hear your testimony, and watch you walk in freedom. But even if I did not see that miracle in this lifetime, I believe with all my heart that God was never finished with you.

I hold on to the truth that His mercy is wider than my reach, deeper than my prayers, and stronger than my love. I believe that seeds of faith were planted in you—truths that could not be uprooted. And I trust that in His mercy, even in your last breath, God was near.

This is not the end. Eternity is long. Heaven is real. I believe we will meet again in the presence of Jesus, with no more sorrow, no more tears, only joy unending. Until then, I will carry hope in my heart, because I know your story is safe in His hands.

Always love you. Always here for you.
[Your Name]

Chapter 23:
Celebrating the Victories:
Their Story Isn't Over

When you love a prodigal, your heart naturally notices every failure. Missed curfews. Broken promises. Another relapse. Another lie. The weight of disappointment becomes so heavy that you start bracing yourself for the next blow. It can feel easier to expect the worst than to risk hoping for change.

But that is not the way of God. He does not keep a scorecard of wrongs.

"Love keeps no record of wrongs" (1 Corinthians 13:5).

If God Himself has chosen not to define your prodigal by their failures, you cannot keep defining them by what went wrong either.

Instead, you are invited into a new posture: celebration. Celebration is not naïve. It does not deny the pain. Celebration is warfare. It declares to the enemy: "You don't get the last word. God does."

Every softened tone, every answered text, every small shift of heart is a victory. These moments may seem insignificant to the world, but they are the fingerprints of God. They are proof that the Spirit is still stirring. They are whispers from heaven: "I'm still here. I'm still working. Their story isn't over."

And here is the truth: if you wait until the finish line to celebrate, you will miss the joy of the journey. God calls you to sing,

124

dance, and rejoice even while the battle rages—because every step forward is evidence that He is still writing.

So don't be a doomsayer. Don't be the one rehearsing failure, saying, "He'll never change… she'll always go back… nothing will ever be different." Those words echo the enemy, not your Father. Instead, rise up as a celebrator. Clap your hands, lift your voice, and declare: "I see God's hand. I see His work. I will praise Him in advance!"

Celebration turns pain into praise. It shifts your eyes from what is broken to the One who is still building. It strengthens your weary soul and reminds the heavens and the earth that your prodigal's story isn't over—it is still unfolding, chapter by chapter, by the hand of God.

Scriptures to Declare

- "This is the day that the Lord has made; let us rejoice and be glad in it." — Psalm 118:24 (ESV)

- "Rejoice in the Lord always; again I will say, rejoice." — Philippians 4:4 (ESV)

- "Love keeps no record of wrongs." — 1 Corinthians 13:5 (NIV)

- "Being confident of this, that He who began a good work in you will carry it on to completion until the day of Christ Jesus." — Philippians 1:6 (NIV)

Practical Guidance

1. **Look for glimmers, not just breakthroughs**
   Notice the small steps: a calmer tone, a text answered, a rare moment of truth. Celebrate them as evidence of God at work.

125

2. **Speak hope out loud**
When despair whispers "never" or "always," respond out loud with faith: "God is still working. Their story isn't over."

3. **Record faithfulness, not failure**
Keep a journal of answered prayers and small victories. Return to it when despair tries to take over.

4. **Celebrate with others**
Share testimonies with trusted friends who will rejoice with you, not criticize.

5. **Let joy fuel perseverance**
Celebration strengthens you for the long journey. Joy is spiritual warfare—it pushes back despair.

Prayer

Father God,

I choose today to lift my eyes above the failures and disappointments and see the signs of life You are stirring. Forgive me for every time I rehearsed despair instead of celebrating hope. Forgive me for speaking words like "never" and "always" that echoed the enemy instead of Your truth.

I declare now: You are faithful. You are working. You will finish what You started in my prodigal's life.

Thank You for the victories, both big and small. Thank You for softened words, for brief moments of honesty, for every flicker of hope that reminds me You are near. Thank You that their mistakes cannot erase Your promises.

Fill me with joy that refuses to be silent—joy that sings in the battle, dances in the waiting, and shouts praise even in the in-between. Let my celebration be a weapon against despair and a reminder to the enemy that he does not get the last word—You do.

In Jesus' name, Amen.

Affirmations

1. I will not keep a record of wrongs—I will keep a record of God's faithfulness.

2. Every small step forward is a sign of God's Spirit at work.

3. My joy is an act of warfare against despair.

4. God is still writing my prodigal's story.

5. I refuse to be a doomsayer—I will be a praiser.

6. Despair will not silence my song; hope will fuel my praise.

7. Every celebration is a declaration: "Their story isn't over."

Prayer Focus

- Praise God daily for His unseen work in your prodigal's life.

- Ask Him to give you eyes to see the small but significant signs of His Spirit.

- Pray for protection against despair and doomsaying, asking God to fill your heart with joy and expectation.

- Choose one physical act of celebration this week—singing, clapping, journaling, or sharing testimony—as a declaration of faith.

A Letter of Eternal Hope

My Dear [Child's/Grandchild's Name],

I want you to know that I don't keep a record of your wrongs, and neither does God. I refuse to define you by your failures, because He has already called you His beloved. Instead, I choose to celebrate every glimmer of hope I see in you—every kind word, every small step forward, every moment that shows God is still working in your life.

This is not the end of your story. Even when it feels slow, even when it looks hard, I believe change is happening. Every step forward matters. Every small victory whispers: "I'm not finished yet."

So I will keep praising God for you. I will keep celebrating you. And I will keep believing that the best chapters of your life are still to come.

Always love you. Always here for you.
[Your Name]

Celebration Anthem: Their Story Isn't Over

High-five the Holy Spirit.
Fall on your knees and thank God.
Clap your hands, dance, and lift your voice in praise.

Because God is still writing. He's still moving. He's still holding both you and your prodigal in His hands.

Don't let despair steal your song. Don't let the enemy silence your praise. Every victory—big or small—is worth celebrating, because every victory declares the truth:

Their story isn't over. And neither is yours.

Epilogue:
You Are Not Alone

If you take only one truth from this book, let it be this: you are not alone.

You are not the only parent or grandparent who has cried through sleepless nights, prayed prayers that seemed unanswered, or carried the ache of watching someone you love walk away from God. Across the world and throughout history, countless mothers, fathers, and grandparents have carried this same burden. And in every generation, God has been faithful.

You are not alone because others are walking this same road right now. There are believers, prayer groups, and faithful friends who will stand with you if you reach out. The enemy wants to isolate you in silence and shame—but God calls you into fellowship, into community, into hope shared together.

Most of all, you are not alone because God Himself walks with you. He is the Father who never gives up on His children. He is the Shepherd who goes after the one lost sheep. He is the Spirit who intercedes with groanings too deep for words when you can no longer pray. He is Emmanuel—God with us.

Your story is still unfolding. Your prodigal's story is still unfolding. God's story is still unfolding. And in the end, His story is always good.

As you close this book, remember: your prayers are powerful, your faith has eternal weight, and your love reflects the heart of

God. You are not alone—you never have been, and you never will be.

The Power of Surrender

There comes a moment in every parent's and grandparent's journey when the prayers feel empty, the waiting feels endless, and the heart feels too heavy to carry another day. That is when God whispers, "Now, give them to Me."

Surrender is not giving up—it is giving over. It is not a declaration of defeat, but a declaration of trust. It is the holy act of releasing the one you love most into the hands of the One who loves them even more.

When you surrender your prodigal, you are saying:

- "God, I trust You more than I trust my own strength."

- "Your timing is better than mine."

- "Your mercy is deeper than my understanding."

It is not easy to open your hands when your heart is breaking. But surrender is not losing your child—it is inviting God to take His rightful place as their Savior. He can go where you cannot go, reach when you have exhausted every reach, and heal what human love cannot fix.

When you finally release the weight of worry, peace flows in like a quiet tide. Your prayers become lighter, your faith steadier, and your spirit freer. You learn to say, "Lord, I still believe, even if I can't see."

Let this be the moment where striving ends and trusting begins. You have prayed, cried, and fought—but now you can rest, knowing the battle belongs to the Lord.

"Be still, and know that I am God." — Psalm 46:10
"Cast all your anxiety on Him because He cares for you."
— 1 Peter 5:7

"The Lord will fight for you; you need only to be still."
— Exodus 14:14

So, breathe. Let go.

Your hands may be empty, but your heart is still full of faith.
And in God's perfect timing—He will write the rest of the story.

A Final Blessing

Father,

I lift up this dear parent and grandparent who has walked through these pages with me. You see the weight they carry, the tears they have cried, and the prayers they have prayed. You know the name of their prodigal, and You love them even more than they do.

Lord, I speak blessing over this family. I declare Your protection, Your peace, and Your promises over every child and grandchild. I break the power of despair and release the power of hope. I silence the lies of the enemy and release the truth of Your Word. I declare that no prayer is wasted, no seed is lost, and no story is too far gone for You to redeem.

May this parent, this grandparent, walk in supernatural strength. May they rest in Your love when the waiting feels long. May their faith be unshakable, their hope unmovable, and their joy unstoppable.

And may their prodigal's story—whether in this lifetime or in eternity—end in redemption, restoration, and glory to Your name.

In the name of the Father, the Son, and the Holy Spirit, Amen.

Their Story Isn't Over Journal

Continuing the Journey

"He who began a good work in you will carry it on to completion until the day of Christ Jesus." — Philippians 1:6

This journal is your sacred space to keep walking with God—through the seasons that follow, the prayers yet to be answered, and the victories still unfolding.

Write freely. Pour out your heart in gratitude, sorrow, and surrender. Record the names you are praying for, the Scriptures you are standing on, and the moments when you sense God's nearness.

Every line you fill becomes another page in the testimony of what God is doing in you—and in the ones you love. Their story isn't over. Neither is yours. And God is faithful to complete what He began.

My Reflections

(Write what God is showing you in this season.)

"The Lord is near to the brokenhearted." — Psalm 34:18

My Prayers for My Prodigal

(Lift their name before God. Record petitions, hopes, and declarations.)

"Before they call I will answer; while they are still speaking I will hear." — Isaiah 65:24

When I See God Move

(Moments—big or small—that remind you He's working.)

"The Lord will fight for you; you need only to be still." — Exodus 14:14

My Praises and Gratitude

(List blessings, provisions, and answered prayers.)

"Give thanks to the Lord, for He is good; His love endures forever."

— Psalm 107:1

Scriptures That Spoke to Me

(Verses that strengthened your faith this week.)

"Your word is a lamp to my feet and a light to my path." — Psalm 119:105

What I've Learned in the Waiting

(Reflections on patience, love, and endurance.)

"Be still before the Lord and wait patiently for Him." — Psalm 37:7

Prayers for My Family

(Lift up peace, unity, and protection for your household.)

"As for me and my house, we will serve the Lord." — Joshua 24:15

139

Signs of Hope

(Describe any changes or softening of hearts you've noticed.)

"Those who sow in tears shall reap with shouts of joy." — Psalm 126:5

My Faith Declaration

(Write your personal statement of trust in God's promises.)

"Let us hold fast the confession of our hope without wavering, for He who promised is faithful." — Hebrews 10:23

Looking Ahead with Hope

(Reflect on how far God has brought you and what you still believe Him to do.)

"For I know the plans I have for you, declares the Lord, plans to prosper you and not to harm you, plans to give you a future and a hope." — Jeremiah 29:11

About the Author

Joanne Beepot is a Real Estate Broker Associate, Kids' Ministry Director, and graduate of Harvard University. She serves faithfully at her church, where her heart for prayer and family restoration has inspired her to help others find lasting hope in Christ.

Joanne's passion is to see families healed and prodigals return home through the power of prayer and God's unfailing love. Drawing from years of ministry and her own journey of intercession, she writes with honesty, compassion, and an unshakable belief that no story is ever too far gone for God to redeem. She loves her family deeply and believes every generation can experience God's transforming grace.

Rooted deeply in her faith, Joanne lives by the promise that "with God all things are possible" (Matthew 19:26). This truth has become the foundation of her ministry and the heartbeat behind every prayer she prays. When faced with moments of discouragement or delay, she clings to another life verse: *"I can do all things through Christ who strengthens me"* (Philippians 4:13). Those words remind her daily to keep on praying, keep on believing, never give up, and surrender everything to her powerful God.

When she's not writing or teaching, Joanne enjoys time with her husband, Al, and their children and grandchildren—the joys of her life and daily reminders of God's grace. She can often be found leading children's Bible classes, cheering at her grandsons' games, or walking along the beach—where she finds peace, purpose, and inspiration in the presence of God.

"No prayer is wasted. God hears every word—even the ones whispered through tears."

Scriptures by Chapter

Part I: The Weight of the Journey

1. When Your Heart Breaks

- "The Lord is near to the brokenhearted and saves the crushed in spirit." — Psalm 34:18
- "He heals the brokenhearted and binds up their wounds." — Psalm 147:3
- "Those who sow in tears shall reap with shouts of joy." — Psalm 126:5
- "Even though I walk through the valley of the shadow of death, I will fear no evil, for You are with me." — Psalm 23:4

2. Trusting God's Perfect Timing

- "For everything there is a season, and a time for every matter under heaven." — Ecclesiastes 3:1
- "Be still before the Lord and wait patiently for Him." — Psalm 37:7
- "The vision awaits its appointed time... If it seems slow, wait for it; it will surely come; it will not delay." — Habakkuk 2:3
- "He has made everything beautiful in its time." — Ecclesiastes 3:11

3. Praying with Authority and Boldness

- "The prayer of a righteous person has great great power as it is working." — James 5:16
- "Let us then with confidence draw near to the throne of grace." — Hebrews 4:16
- "Truly I tell you, if you have faith and do not doubt... it will

be done." — Matthew 21:21–22
- "Whatever you ask in My name, this I will do." — John 14:13–14

4. Battling Shame, Blame, and Condemnation

- "There is therefore now no condemnation for those who are in Christ Jesus." — Romans 8:1
- "Those who look to Him are radiant; their faces shall never be ashamed." — Psalm 34:5
- "As far as the east is from the west, so far does He remove our transgressions from us." — Psalm 103:12
- "My grace is sufficient for you, for My power is made perfect in weakness." — 2 Corinthians 12:9

5. When You Feel Like Giving Up

- "Those who hope in the Lord will renew their strength." — Isaiah 40:31
- "Do not grow weary in doing good, for in due season we will reap if we do not give up." — Galatians 6:9
- "The Lord will fight for you; you need only to be still." — Exodus 14:14
- "Weeping may last for the night, but joy comes in the morning." — Psalm 30:5

Part II: The Hard Realities

6. When Prodigals Are Addicted, Abusive, or Mentally Bound

- "The Spirit of the Lord is upon Me... to proclaim liberty to the captives." — Luke 4:18
- "The Lord is my strength and my defense; He has become my salvation." — Exodus 15:2
- "No weapon that is fashioned against you shall succeed." — Isaiah 54:17
- "The Lord is faithful; He will establish you and guard you from the evil one." — 2 Thessalonians 3:3

7. When Prodigals Disrupt the Family

- "Peace I leave with you; My peace I give to you." — John 14:27
- "The prudent sees danger and hides himself." — Proverbs 22:3
- "If possible, so far as it depends on you, live peaceably with all." — Romans 12:18
- "You will keep in perfect peace those whose minds are steadfast." — Isaiah 26:3

8. When Prodigals Make Life-Altering Choices

- "He will give a crown of beauty for ashes." — Isaiah 61:3
- "We know that in all things God works for the good of those who love Him." — Romans 8:28
- "For I know the plans I have for you." — Jeremiah 29:11
- "Nothing will be impossible with God." — Luke 1:37

9. When They Don't See Their Need for God

- "The god of this world has blinded the minds of the unbelievers." — 2 Corinthians 4:4
- "I will remove the heart of stone and give you a heart of flesh." — Ezekiel 36:26
- "For the Son of Man came to seek and to save the lost." — Luke 19:10
- "The Lord is not slow to fulfill His promise... but patient toward you." — 2 Peter 3:9

10. Communicating with Prodigals

- "Let your speech always be gracious, seasoned with salt." — Colossians 4:6
- "A soft answer turns away wrath, but a harsh word stirs up anger." — Proverbs 15:1
- "Be quick to hear, slow to speak, slow to anger." — James 1:19
- "Do everything in love." — 1 Corinthians 16:14

11. When Prodigals Threaten to Harm Themselves or Others

• "The Lord is near to the brokenhearted and saves the crushed in spirit." — Psalm 34:18
• "He will command His angels concerning you to guard you in all your ways." — Psalm 91:11
• "When you pass through the waters, I will be with you." — Isaiah 43:2
• "The name of the Lord is a strong tower; the righteous run into it and are safe." — Proverbs 18:10

12. Facing Public Shame and Judgment

• "The Lord is my light and my salvation—whom shall I fear?" — Psalm 27:1
• "The fear of man lays a snare, but whoever trusts in the Lord is safe." — Proverbs 29:25
• "Those who hope in the Lord will never be put to shame." — Isaiah 49:23
• "Blessed are those who are persecuted for righteousness' sake." — Matthew 5:10

Part III: Fighting the Battle

13. Engaging in Spiritual Warfare

• "Be strong in the Lord and in the strength of His might." — Ephesians 6:10
• "Put on the full armor of God." — Ephesians 6:11
• "The weapons of our warfare are not of the flesh but have divine power." — 2 Corinthians 10:4
• "Resist the devil, and he will flee from you." — James 4:7

14. Breaking Curses, Releasing Promises for Generations

• "Christ redeemed us from the curse." — Galatians 3:13
• "He keeps His covenant of love to a thousand generations." — Deuteronomy 7:9
• "The steadfast love of the Lord is from everlasting to everlasting." — Psalm 103:17
• "No weapon formed against you shall prosper." — Isaiah 54:17

15. Holding On to Hope

- "May the God of hope fill you with all joy and peace in believing." — Romans 15:13
- "We have this hope as an anchor for the soul." — Hebrews 6:19
- "Let us hold fast the confession of our hope without wavering." — Hebrews 10:23
- "The Lord will fulfill His purpose for me." — Psalm 138:8

16. The Power of Community

- "Two are better than one... if either falls, one can help the other up." — Ecclesiastes 4:9–10
- "Encourage one another and build each other up." — 1 Thessalonians 5:11
- "Carry each other's burdens." — Galatians 6:2
- "Where two or three gather in My name, there am I among them." — Matthew 18:20

17. The God Who Redeems

- "He makes everything beautiful in its time." — Ecclesiastes 3:11
- "The Lord your God is in your midst, a mighty one who will save." — Zephaniah 3:17
- "He restores my soul." — Psalm 23:3
- "Behold, I am making all things new." — Revelation 21:5

Part IV: Living Beyond the Waiting

18. Leaving a Legacy of Faith

- "From generation to generation we will proclaim Your faithfulness." — Psalm 79:13
- "Teach them diligently to your children." — Deuteronomy 6:7
- "The righteous who walks in his integrity—blessed are his children after him." — Proverbs 20:7
- "Your faithfulness continues through all generations." — Psalm 119:90

19. A Future and a Hope

- "For I know the plans I have for you." — Jeremiah 29:11
- "Surely goodness and mercy shall follow me." — Psalm 23:6
- "The path of the righteous is like the morning sun." — Proverbs 4:18
- "God is able to do exceedingly abundantly above all we ask or think." — Ephesians 3:20

20. When the Prodigal Doesn't Return Home

- "I shall go to him, but he will not return to me." — 2 Samuel 12:23
- "He will wipe away every tear from their eyes." — Revelation 21:4
- "Blessed are those who mourn, for they shall be comforted." — Matthew 5:4
- "Precious in the sight of the Lord is the death of His saints." — Psalm 116:15

21. Caring for Yourself in the Journey

- "Come to Me, all you who are weary and burdened." — Matthew 11:28
- "He restores my soul." — Psalm 23:3
- "The joy of the Lord is my strength." — Nehemiah 8:10
- "Cast all your anxiety on Him because He cares for you." — 1 Peter 5:7

22. What We Carry Forward

- "Forget the former things; do not dwell on the past." — Isaiah 43:18–19
- "The Lord will fight for you; you need only to be still." — Exodus 14:14
- "He who began a good work in you will carry it to completion." — Philippians 1:6
- "Behold, I am doing a new thing." — Isaiah 43:19

23. Celebrating the Victories

- "This is the day that the Lord has made; let us rejoice and be glad in it." — Psalm 118:24
- "Rejoice in the Lord always; again I will say, rejoice." — Philippians 4:4
- "Love keeps no record of wrongs." — 1 Corinthians 13:5
- "He who promised is faithful." — Hebrews 10:23

Affirmations by Chapter

Part I: The Weight of the Journey

1. When Your Heart Breaks

1. God is near to the brokenhearted.
2. My tears are seen, my prayers are heard, and my hope is not lost.
3. Even in pain, I will trust the One who holds both me and my prodigal.
4. Healing has already begun, even if I cannot yet see it.
5. God's love reaches deeper than my heartbreak.

2. Trusting God's Perfect Timing

1. God's timing is not late; it is holy and right.
2. Waiting is not wasted when I wait with faith.
3. My prodigal's story is unfolding according to God's design.
4. I can rest because God is still working behind the scenes.
5. I release control and choose to trust the Author of time itself.

3. Praying with Authority and Boldness

1. My prayers are powerful because God listens.
2. I speak life, not fear, over my prodigal.
3. I have spiritual authority through Jesus Christ.
4. Heaven hears my voice when I pray in faith.
5. I will not shrink back—I will stand and declare God's promises.

4. Battling Shame, Blame, and Condemnation

1. I refuse to wear shame for someone else's choices.

2. There is no condemnation for those in Christ Jesus.
3. God's grace covers every regret and every "what if."
4. I will not let guilt silence my prayers.
5. The cross has the final word—my family is covered in mercy.

5. When You Feel Like Giving Up

1. I may feel weary, but I will not quit.
2. God's strength rises in my weakness.
3. Hope lives because Jesus lives.
4. My breakthrough may be one prayer away.
5. I will stand firm until I see God's promises fulfilled.

Part II: The Hard Realities

6. When Prodigals Are Addicted, Abusive, or Mentally Bound

1. My home belongs to God and His peace will rule here.
2. Love does not mean enabling; wisdom sets boundaries.
3. No addiction is stronger than the name of Jesus.
4. I am called to be a light, not a doormat.
5. God's mercy can reach where my influence cannot.

7. When Prodigals Disrupt the Family

1. The Prince of Peace reigns over my home.
2. I can love with truth and protect with wisdom.
3. God's peace is stronger than chaos.
4. No weapon formed against my family will prosper.
5. I trust God to bring order, healing, and restoration.

8. When Prodigals Make Life-Altering Choices

1. God can redeem even irreversible choices.
2. No mistake cancels God's mercy.
3. I can love without rescuing and pray without enabling.
4. What the enemy meant for harm, God will turn to good.
5. Every scar can become a testimony of grace.

9. When They Don't See Their Need for God

1. Spiritual blindness cannot outlast God's light.
2. Pride is no match for His mercy.

3. God is still pursuing my prodigal.
4. Their anger cannot push away God's love.
5. The scales will fall—their eyes will see the truth.

10. Communicating with Prodigals

1. I speak truth with grace.
2. My words can sow peace.
3. God can use even silence to speak love.
4. I will listen more and argue less.
5. My tone can reflect God's heart.

11. Affirmations for When Prodigals Are in Crisis

1. I will pray with faith and act with wisdom.
2. God's protection is greater than my fear.
3. I choose courage over panic.
4. My prodigal's life is covered by God's mercy.
5. Even in crisis, I will not lose hope.

12. Facing Public Shame and Judgment

1. My worth is not determined by others' opinions.
2. I am not alone—God stands beside me.
3. My reputation rests in Christ, not the crowd.
4. I will walk with my head high in God's grace.
5. Others' opinions cannot limit what God will do.

Part III: Fighting the Battle

13. Engaging in Spiritual Warfare

1. The battle belongs to the Lord.
2. I fight from victory.
3. Every prayer pushes back the darkness.
4. God's Word is my weapon.
5. Angels are on assignment for my family.

14. Breaking Curses, Releasing Promises

1. The curse stops here; the blessing begins here.
2. My family line is marked for freedom.
3. Jesus has broken every chain.
4. Generational blessing is my inheritance.

5. My prayers echo into future generations.

15. Holding On to Hope

1. Hope is my anchor.
2. I choose faith over fear.
3. I see God's goodness even in delay.
4. My hope rests in His faithfulness.
5. What He started, He will finish.

16. The Power of Community

1. I am not meant to walk alone.
2. God uses others to strengthen me.
3. Shared love multiplies hope.
4. I will give and receive encouragement.
5. Community defeats isolation.

17. The God Who Redeems

1. Nothing is beyond God's redemption.
2. His grace reaches the deepest pit.
3. God restores what was lost.
4. Beauty will rise from ashes.
5. My prodigal's story will declare His goodness.

Part IV: Living Beyond the Waiting

18. Leaving a Legacy of Faith

1. My prayers will outlive me.
2. Faith is the greatest inheritance I can leave.
3. The next generation will rise strong in Christ.
4. My example plants seeds heaven will water.
5. God's promises extend to my children's children.

19. A Future and a Hope

1. God's plans for my family are good.
2. He is not finished with our story.
3. I refuse to fear tomorrow.
4. Every delay is part of His design.
5. My future is secure in His hands.

20. When the Prodigal Doesn't Return Home

1. Even when I don't understand, I will still trust.
2. Death does not have the final word.
3. Heaven holds what earth could not restore.
4. My faith reaches beyond the grave.
5. I will see my prodigal in eternity.

21. Caring for Yourself in the Journey

1. Rest is not weakness—it is worship.
2. God cares for me deeply.
3. My soul matters to Him.
4. I will breathe, heal, and trust again.
5. God renews my strength daily.

22. What We Carry Forward

1. I am not who I once was.
2. God has refined my faith through fire.
3. I carry peace, not pain.
4. Gratitude is my testimony.
5. The story continues—with hope.

23. Celebrating the Victories

1. I will rejoice in every sign of change.
2. God deserves praise even in progress.
3. Celebration silences despair.
4. My joy is my weapon.
5. Their story—and mine—isn't over.

Practical Tools for the Journey

- **Keep a Prayer Journal** – Record prayers, answered requests, and spiritual milestones.
- **Create an Ebenezer Jar** – Write answered prayers or moments of breakthrough on small stones or papers as reminders of God's faithfulness.
- **Form a Prayer Circle** – Partner with two or three trusted believers who commit to intercede weekly.
- **Use Scripture Declarations** – Speak God's promises aloud daily over your prodigal's life.
- **Establish a "Day of Hope" Tradition** – Choose one day each month to fast, worship, and pray specifically for prodigals.
- **Set a "Family Faith Table"** – Dedicate a small space for Scripture cards, answered prayer notes, or legacy items.
- **Create a Family Blessing Book** – Write down blessings for future generations to read and add to.
- **Engage in Soul-Care Practices** – Prayer walks, worship playlists, journaling, and gratitude lists can strengthen your spirit in weary seasons.

Your Story Isn't Over

I watch you wander, far away,
Your laughter faded, your light turned gray.
I call your name in whispered prayer,
Hoping somehow you'll feel I'm there.

I've wept on pillows soaked in night,
I've begged the Lord to make it right.
I'd take the pain, I'd trade the cost,
If it would mean you'd not be lost.

But when my prayers reach Heaven's throne,
I hear a voice—*You're not alone.*
The One who formed you, breathed your days, Speaks to my heart
in tender ways:

God's Voice:

*"My child is wandering, yes, I see,
But no one loves them more than Me.
Their story's ink is not yet dry,
I've marked their soul, they can't deny.

I walk the roads they choose at night,
I chase them down with holy light.
Through smoke, through shame, through bitter tears,
I've carried them through hidden years.

You think they're gone, beyond repair,
But I am God—I'll meet them there.
No chain too strong, no pit too deep,
No lost one I cannot keep.

157

So lift your eyes, release your fear,
Their ending hasn't written here.
What you call ruined, I call mine,
And I'll redeem it, in My time."*

So I will trust, though I can't see,
The God who's greater still than me.
My prodigal may roam and roam,
But Heaven's arms will bring them home.

And when that day of mercy comes,
The Father runs, the child undone.
The robe, the ring, the feast, the song—
The story ends where it belongs.

A Note from the Author

Thank you for walking through these pages with me. Writing Their Story Isn't Over has been both a journey of tears and a journey of hope—because like you, I know the heartbreak of loving a prodigal. I have prayed prayers that felt unanswered, carried burdens that felt too heavy, and asked God questions that only a hurting parent or grandparent can understand.

This book was born out of real life—out of sleepless nights, whispered prayers, and moments when faith felt like the only thing left to hold. But more than that, it was born out of God's faithfulness. Over and over, He met me in the waiting. He lifted me when I was weary. He reminded me that His mercy does not run out, His promises do not fail, and His story is not finished.

If there's one truth I want you to carry with you, it's this: your prayers matter. Your faith has eternal weight. Your tears are not wasted. Every whispered prayer, every sleepless night, and every act of love sown in faith is seen and treasured by God.

You are not alone—not in your waiting, not in your pain, and not in your hope. Whether your prodigal is far away, making painful choices, or even if they never returned in this life, God is near to you. He sees you. He loves you. And He is still working behind the scenes in ways you cannot yet see.

As you close this book, may you carry forward a deeper faith, a stronger hope, and an unshakable confidence that the God who began this story will finish it.

Because no matter what it looks like today—their story isn't over.

And neither is yours.

With love, prayer, and faith,

Joanne Beepot

159

May God restore every wandering heart and bring peace to every waiting soul.

www.ingramcontent.com/pod-product-compliance
Lightning Source LLC
Chambersburg PA
CBHW030301130626
46549CB00002B/637